Brainswitching: Learning on the Right Side of the Brain

Fast, Stress-Free Access
to Languages, Mathematics,
Science, and much,
much more!

SECOND EDITION

by
James J. Asher, Ph.D.

Prize-winning Writer & Educator,
Originator of the Total Physical Response,
known worldwide as TPR

Brainswitching: Learning on the Right Side of the Brain

Fast, Stress-Free Access
to Languages, Mathematics,
Science, and much, much more!

by
James J. Asher, Ph.D.

Prize-winning Writer & Educator,
Originator of the Total Physical Response,
known worldwide as TPR

First Edition ISBN: 0-940296-57-8
Second Edition ISBN: 1-56018-036-6

Published by
Sky Oaks Productions, Inc.
P.O. Box 1102
Los Gatos, California 95031 USA
Phone: (408) 395-7600   Fax: (408) 395-8440
e-mail: **tprworld@aol.com**

To order other books by Dr. Asher, click on:
www.tpr-world.com

© Copyright 1988, 2001

TABLE OF CONTENTS

Chapter 2 (Continued)

Chapter 3: Illusions
(The logic of the left brain) 3-1

Chapter 3 (Continued)

Chapter 5 (Continued)

Chapter 6: The selection interview 6-1

Chapter 8 (Continued)

Chapter 9: Use brainswitching to learn the second most difficult subject in school 9-1

Chapter 9 (Continued)

Chapter 10: Use brainswitching to learn the most difficult subject in school 10-1

ACKNOWLEDGMENTS

When Dr. Roger Sperry conducted his Nobel prize-winning experiment with cats that demonstrated for the first time in the laboratory that each side of the brain is able to process information independently, he had no inkling that he would inspire 4,000 follow-up studies of brain laterality by researchers around the world. We now know more about the characteristics of each hemisphere of the brain than all other organs in the body put together.

DEDICATION

First Edition

"There is a lesson to be learned here..."

In memory of Norman Asher Sr. and Norman Asher, Jr.

Second Edition

"Go to him, talk to him, win him over..."

In memory of James J. Asher, Sr.

PREFACE TO THE FIRST EDITION

Since the first successful demonstration by Nobel Laureate Roger Sperry that each hemisphere of the brain can process information independently, hundreds of follow-up studies have been conducted by every scientific specialist from psychologists to biochemists, from linguists to anthropologists, from research physicians to speech pathologists. A few years ago, from every discipline, scholars who researched the dual brain, gathered at UCLA in Los Angeles, California for a three-day conference to compare notes. (Benson and Zaidel, 1985).

A clearer picture is developing about how each hemisphere of the brain processes incoming raw data and transforms the input into information. In this book I have attempted to achieve two goals: The first is to reinterpret, using the dual brain model, studies in selected areas of psychology such as hypnosis, visual illusions, learning, problem solving, therapy and others because the concept of a double brain gives us a fresh perspective of puzzling problems in human behavior.

My second goal is to apply the concept of a dual brain to solving practical problems in language acquisition, mathematics, counseling, personnel selection and others. I believe that solving problems in practical areas of human activity can be more effective with what I call, **brainswitching** which means skillfully moving information from one side of the brain to the other and back again.

Educators are aware of dual brain research but view this development as an interesting curio which someday may have practical application to instruction. Throughout this book, I shall demonstrate that brainswitching has rich applications for solving problems today. Also, you will see that I personally apply brainswitching in each chapter by *alternating* from a concept (input to the left brain) to a story (input to the right brain).

As a caveat, the technical literature concerning the brain is exploratory and suggestive rather than "laws" cast in bronze. In other words, the concept of a dual brain should be viewed as an approximation — a tentative picture of brain function.

As I sat through the three-day conference of dual brain researchers at UCLA, I frankly wondered as I listened to the kaleidoscope of technical presentations whether the split-brain was a fashionable scientific fantasy or indeed had a factual basis.

Finally, at the climax of the three-day paper-reading session, Dr. Joseph Bogan who did the original surgery to separate the corpus callosum in humans, walked to the podium in the huge auditorium and said*, ". . . you know, listening to paper after paper presented by researchers from so many different disciplines, I honestly began to wonder whether the dual brain was science fiction or had some solid basis in reality.

"Then, during the lunch break I visited a gentleman who is a patient at the UCLA Medical School. This man had a left hemispherectomy (the entire left hemisphere has been removed surgically) so that he is unable to utter one word. Yet, when you ask him to sing, he can sing an aria like Caruso. Listening to him sing, I said to myself, 'There has to be something to this left brain-right brain business.' "

*I have paraphrased Dr. Bogan's speech.

PREFACE TO THE SECOND EDITION

The picture of how each hemisphere of the brain processes information has not changed since the first edition of this book. It is now established that the brain processes information ahead (and faster than) our awareness and knows "the answer" at least a half second before we do.

I still believe that when we ask our right brain for "an answer," that hemisphere of the brain will continue to search within its vast filing system. It will simultaneously scan on a kind of "radar screen" things coming in from the outside that we see, hear, feel, touch, and smell—in a continuous effort to develop "an answer" that we will accept as a solution. Unless and until we direct the right brain to stop the search with comments such as *"I give up!"* or *"I guess there is no solution,"* the right brain will compute, compute, and compute.

When Sir Isaac Newton was asked how he got his remarkable insights into the secrets of gravity, he said: *"By always thinking about it. By always having it in front of me."* Most people do not know that Sir Isaac entered Cambridge at the age of 19 with little more mathematical skill than simple arithmetic. Yet, when he needed mathematics that did not exist in the 17th century to solve the gravitational relationships between planets, he accessed his right brain to discover a new mathematical procedure called "calculus." I like Dr. Albert Einstein's comment that *"imagination* (on the right side of the brain) *is more important than intelligence."* Amazingly, when little Albert was a boy and his father asked the headmaster of the school what kind of education he recommended for his son, the reply was, *"It doesn't matter. He will not succeed at anything he does."*

As a simple test you can do at home to test the remarkable power of your brain, ask your right brain: *"What is the name of every teacher I had in school from kindergarten through high school?"* It helps to write down the question so that the right brain can read it. Remember, even though the right brain is mute, it can hear and it can read. Let me know what happens. My e-mail is tprworld@aol.com

WHAT'S NEW IN THIS EDITION

CHAPTER 9:
USE BRAINSWITCHING TO LEARN THE SECOND MOST DIFFICULT SUBJECT IN SCHOOL

Nowhere are the differences between the left and right brain more visible than in mathematical education. Remember, in the U.S.A., we spend more money on remedial mathematics than all other forms of math education put together. Something is not working. My office partner, who was a college tennis champion, once told me that his tennis coach used to say when the game was not going well, "Do something different!"

An interesting example of how the left and right brain works in students is to look at word problems in algebra. The assumption is that word problems improve "problem solving, creativity and thinking." There is no evidence that solving those word problems transfers to other intellectual skills such as problem solving, creativity, or thinking. Solving those word problems only makes one proficient at solving more word problems exactly like those in the textbook. But, for the moment let's accept that word problems are a good exercise for students.

A CLOSER LOOK AT WORD PROBLEMS

Seventh-graders were asked to solve this word problem: "Orville and Wilbur owned a bicycle shop which also sold tricycles. One day, they decided to take an inventory of their stock. They each volunteered to count one item, which would have worked out just fine if one had counted bicycles and the other had counted tricycles. But Orville and Wilbur were both very independent thinkers. Orville counted the number of pedals in the shop and Wilbur counted the number of wheels.

"Orville found that they had 144 pedals in the shop, and Wilbur found that they had 186 wheels. All pedals and wheels were actually parts of either bicycles or tricycles. They were just about to start over with their inventory when their friend Kitty, who was a good problem solver, challenged them to figure out the number of bicycles and tricycles from the inventory they had already done. Can you help the Wright brothers? How many bicycles and tricycles did they have in their shop?..." *(San Jose Mercury News, April 3, 1995)*.

Some kids perceive this as a fun puzzle and joyfully speculated about possible ways to develop an answer. Other youngsters perceive this word problem as absolute nonsense.

They reason: We are talking about the Wright brothers, owners of a bicycle shop in Ohio. The brothers are famous for doing the impossible—inventing a bicycle that flies in the air. Secondly, these thoughtful students (who probably will get "F" in algebra) do not believe that the geniuses who invented the airplane would waste valuable hours counting wheels and pedals when the simple solution is to count bicycles and tricycles. Surely these intellectual giants have something better to do with their time. The group of thoughtful students will be among the 50% who become casualties—math dysfunctionals who view themselves for the rest of their lives as, "No good in math."

An instructor with a solid conceptual model of how each side of the brain works can anticipate what is going on in the student's mind and neutralize self-destructive brain messages. For example, "I know what many of you are thinking. You are thinking that this is nonsense because ... Instead, think of this as a little puzzle which can be fun to decode like cracking the secret code used by spies in wartime." *

As a special bonus, in Chapter 9, you will also discover an intriguing right brain revelation that may solve the mystery of multiplying negative numbers. Thoughtful students in a traditional algebra class reason like this: We know that 2 plus 2 equals a +4 and a (-2) plus a (-2) equals a -4. If that is so and multiplication is simply repeated addition, then if 2 time 2 equals a +4, why isn't (-2) times a (-2) equal to a -4 ? Well, maybe it is. Get ready for a surprising discovery.

CHAPTER 10:
USE BRAINSWITCHING TO LEARN
THE MOST DIFFICULT SUBJECT IN SCHOOL

In the first edition (1988), I reported on my right brain strategy for learning a second language that gives students of all ages instant understanding of any target language. The benefits of this strategy are stress-free learning, self- confidence for the instructor and the students, and long-term retention. I call this strategy the Total Physical Response, known worldwide as TPR.

Now, in the second edition (2001), I report another breakthrough based on my original research, that takes students from understanding the target language in the first exposure to developing skill in speaking, reading and writing. Instead of only 5% of students in traditional classes experiencing success in acquiring another language, the success rate climbs to a spectacular 95%. This new strategy is called TPR Storytelling (TPRS).

*See *Learning Algebra on the Right Side of the Brain*
by James J. Asher (*To read the article, click on www.tpr-world.com*)

Chapter 1: The Brain's Landscape

I created the word, **brainswitching** to represent a new skill which is to communicate more effectively by **alternating** information processing through the right and left hemispheres of the brain. Professor Roger Sperry of the California Institute of Technology has demonstrated in his Nobel prize-winning experiments that each hemisphere of the brain can process information independently.

Professor Sperry's discovery of a dual brain (which has been a topic of speculation and theorizing for several centuries by philosophers, physiologists and neurologists) is perhaps the most exciting finding in the behavioral sciences in our generation. The reason: Not only is each hemisphere of the brain capable of independently processing information, but follow-up studies by other researchers suggest that each side of the brain is sensitive to different input coming into the sensory receptors. That is, each side of the brain may hear, see, and understand different messages coming from the outside.

In ordinary everyday situations, both sides of the brain are alternating — usually at lightning-speed — to process information. The velocity is so fast that we are almost instantly brainswitching. This may be happening continuously and so rapidly that it is not usually within our awareness. For example, a few days ago, I asked a stranger on the street, "Can you give me directions to the Alameda tunnel?" I noticed the person's body movements when he answered. The head and eyes moved in a particular direction, and an arm, hand and finger was pointed as a navigational aid. The person spoke (which turns on the left brain) but then there was a rich mosaic of body movements (which turns on the right brain).

The person giving directions will talk and gesture which is an attempt to alternate rapidly between the left and right hemispheres of the brain to assemble an intelligent, coherent answer. As an experiment, if you were to ask the question about directions to a location and someone else was to restrain the stranger's body motions by holding the person, it would be extremely difficult for the individual to formulate an accurate answer because only one-half of the brain — the left hemisphere would be switched on and functioning.

Professor Sperry's double-brain demonstration (and the follow-up research by others) implies that (a) each hemisphere can function independently, (b) each hemisphere may process information differently, (c) one hemisphere communicates with the other at lightning-speed, (d) messages may flicker back-and-forth from one hemisphere to the other continuously, and (e) inter-hemispheric communication is usually too fast for us to register in awareness.

But there is more. If all this is true, and I believe it is, then most experiments in the behavioral sciences such as those in learning, hypnosis and therapy will have to be reevaluated because when the research data were collected initially, researchers were not aware that how subjects **were asked to respond** will make a dramatic difference in the results of the experiment. For example, if the double-brain hypothesis is correct, then different sides of the brain will be turned-on when the subject is asked to read, speak, write, draw, gesture, act, or sing. The mode of response will have a crucial impact on results.

To give a specific example, most studies of human learning by psychologists in the past one hundred years (with the exception of the Gestaltists) have used **verbal materials.** Hence, subjects in those research studies typically were asked to read something and write something. If not reading and writing, then reading and speaking.

Since reading, writing and speaking are activities of the left brain, the conclusions about acquisition and retention (that is, learning and memory) are "laws" for left brain functioning. The learning research which is the basis of modern educational psychology applies to only half of the brain, the left hemisphere.

The concept of the brain before Sperry's demonstration

Historically, brain scientists believed that the brain was symmetrical. This seemed logical because it was consistent with organs in the body. For example, if you examine medical illustrations, the symmetry of the human anatomy is more striking than subtle asymmetries — and, no organs in the human body appear to the naked eye to be more symmetrical than the brain. Other organs, although they may appear to have an asymmetrical appearance, were thought to be merely mirror images of each other since the function of each was identical.

For example, the right and left lungs are not only easily differentiated when you look at them, but they do not even have the same number of major divisions

(Benson, 1985). Yet, the right and left lung have an identical function. What is true of the lungs also applies to the kidneys, the thyroid glands, the reproductive glands, eyes, ears, arms, and legs. Why was it not reasonable to conclude that each hemisphere of the brain had an identical function?

To further solidify the holistic concept of the brain, human mental functions were discussed by philosophers and academicians as products of the mind. For instance, psychologists developed the famous concept of intelligence as a product of a holistic entity called the mind. Statistically, something called General Intelligence was identified early in the exploration of mental ability using the novel measurement called, the intelligence test. However, components of Specific Intelligence were also identified. Hence, the view was that there is both general and specific intelligence operating in each person and animal.

Although the prevailing tendency was to conceptualize the brain functioning as a holistic entity, there were, curiously enough, speculations about a dual brain that go back at least 2,000 years (Benson, 1985). The notion was that going from the front to the rear of the brain, different locations carried out specialized functions such as perception. reasoning, and memory.

It wasn't until 1761 that Morgagni in Italy showed that localized brain function was possible by demonstrating cross innervation — which means that when one side of the brain was stimulated, the other side of the body responded. A hundred years later in 1872, an English scientist named Meynert was successful in showing that motor and sensory functions were localized in areas from the front to the back of the brain.

These findings were not persuasive enough, however, to inspire a shift in thinking of the brain as a holistic entity to a picture of the brain as being localized in function.

Evidence for brain localization

The most dramatic evidence of brain localization was developed by Paul Broca in France circa 1865. Broca and his contemporaries presented overwhelming clinical data that the left hemisphere of the brain played a dominant role in language. The observations were based upon the "correlation" of language dysfunctions such as aphasia with lesions in the brain. The neurologist, D. Frank Benson from the UCLA School of Medicine, cites Broca's work as a major intellectual discovery of the 19th century — a contribution that ranks with Darwin's theory of evolution and Freud's demonstration of the unconscious level in human thinking.

It is interesting that for one hundred years after Broca's discovery, physicians used Broca's concept of language localized in the left brain for treating aphasia and other disorders of speech, but they did not believe that this fact indicated a difference between the brain hemispheres. Novel observations in science often take several generations before the implications are understood and utilized. For example, to explore cell physiology, only recent generations of neuroanatomists have used *silver-staining* when this remarkable technique was discovered a hundred years ago by Golgi (1883) and Ramon y Cajal (1928).

As recently as 1950, physiological psychologists from The Johns Hopkins University, commented in a well-known textbook called *Physiological Psychology.*— " . . . It is hard to believe...that the brain is so organized that it has memories for speech in one place and those for music in another. Yet many neurologists believe their evidence indicates that . . ." (p. 515, Morgan and Stellar). The prevailing opinion was that mass action explains most mental functions in the brain.

The evidence for mass action

Mass action means that the brain functions as one integrated, organized entity. Furthermore, there is a phenomenon called *vicarious function* which implies that almost any part of the brain can take over a function if necessary, for another part of the brain that is damaged. Studies of laboratory animals suggested that no matter where in the brain a lesion was placed, there was no difference in the impact on the rate of learning by the animals. For example, Ghiselli (1938) found a correlation of .80 between the size of the lesion and the impairment of learning in animals, but a zero relationship between the location of the lesion and the animals' learning performance.

In other words, the larger the size of the lesion, the more the animal's learning was impaired. Furthermore, Ghiselli showed that where the lesion was located in the brain had no apparent affect upon learning. This seemed to verify Maier's observation in 1932 that the size of lesions (and no*t* location in the brain) produced marked differences in the ability of rats to solve "reasoning" problems.

Vicarious Function

Karl Lashley, the Harvard scientist who was Roger Sperry's mentor, enriched the concept of vicarious function with another intriguing idea: the *equipotentiality of a system.* Lashley believed that within a particular system, one part of the brain could take over for another part that was damaged. Vicarious function, according to Lashley, operated only within a specific system of the brain and not between different systems.

For example, Lashley examined the cases of 18 people who had lesions in the "speech area" of the brain and discovered a remarkable correlation of .90 (remember that 1 is a perfect correlation) between the size of the lesions and the later recovery of the people from aphasia. This means, of course, that the smaller the lesion in the part of the brain associated with the speech system, the faster the person recovered from the linguistic disorder. The implication is that if there is a tear in the brain which disables performance, the remainder of the brain assigned to that function can somehow repair itself to bring performance back to "normal." The more exaggerated the tear, the longer time will be needed to make repairs.*

Other researchers observed similar relationships for the paralysis of motor behavior. The picture of the brain being divided up into different areas that are assigned

*An alternate hypothesis is that the brain is able to **find** or even **create** alternative routes around the damaged area.

For example, see articles on the brain scans of 600 hydrocephalic patients by the British neurologist, Dr. John Lorber. The conclusion: "There must be a tremendous amount of redundancy or space capacity in the brain . . ." (p. 1233, 1980) since with only a thin layer of brain tissue — less than a millimeter compared with a normal brain thickness of 4.5-centimeters, many patients are able to function normally as university students.

As further evidence for the amazing plasticity of the brain, Dr. Lorber observes that laboratory rats can also function normally with huge lesions in the brain if the damage is introduced gradually in a small step-by-step progression.

to do different functions is documented over and over in every chapter of any standard neuroanatomy text. For example, consider an area of the brain called the precentral gyrus (sometimes known as the motor area). Within that area of the brain, a certain space seems to control the leg, another space the arm, another the trunk and still another the face.

A curious fact is that the space within the motor area for the movement of the leg, for instance, is not equal to the space that controls the face. The brain has been meticulously mapped by researchers who electrically stimulated thousands of points on the cerebral landscape and then observed which part of the body responded.

If we were to trace a picture of ourselves as it is represented in the brain, we would look rather like the grotesque person you see in Figure 1 in which our hands are like baseball gloves while our feet are diminutive and almost toeless. Like a prisoner of war, our chest appears emaciated and we have stick-like arms and legs, but we have on the brain-map, a huge mouth, small nose, and a tongue that is almost as large as our face.

Notice that space in the motor area reserved for parts of the body seem to correspond to the sensitivity and control we have for a body-part. For example, our hands occupy many times more space than our feet — and notice that we have huge thumbs with clearly differentiated fingers, but, except for our big toe, the entire foot, including other toes, are merely elongated stubs. Our hands, as represented in the brain's motor area, are baseball gloves each one of which is almost as large as the trunk of the body.

Figure 1

Notice also that our tongue occupies almost as much space in the brain as the entire face. The principle seems to be that the more refined the skilled movement — that is, the greater the precision of the movement, the more space allocated in the brain. When you examine the brain map of the head, certain body-parts that control fine-tuned, precise movements such as vision, speech, and manual manipulation occupy the lion's share of cerebral space. (Notice that ears and hair are almost non-existent on the brain map.)

Now, what happens when there is a tear in the motor area? If the damage is on the left side of the motor cortex, then there will be paralysis on the right side of the body because the neural wiring coming from and to the brain is crossed — that is, the wiring from the left hemisphere travels to the right side of the body and wiring on the right hemisphere is connected to the left side of the body. Furthermore, the paralysis is rather specific. For instance, if the lesion is in the motor area reserved for the arm in the left hemisphere, then the paralysis will occur in the right arm.

Recovery of function for the right arm is intriguing because the first to recover will be locomotion — that is, movement of the arm and later, much later, there is recovery in the ability to manipulate objects (i.e., picking up a pencil, typing, and holding a spoon). Gross movements come back first, then precision movements.

The fascinating conclusion is this: If the **entire** motor area is removed in either primates or humans, there is almost always no recovery of function, but if only a part of the motor area is damaged, then the remaining portion is able apparently to make repairs so that function gradually returns. Incidentally, recovery will be less in humans than in chimpanzees, and less in chimpanzees than monkeys.

MAP OF THE BRAIN BEFORE SPERRY

Before Roger Sperry's demonstration that each hemisphere of the brain could function independently, a compartmentalized cerebral cortex was pictured in almost every chapter of standard physiology textbooks. Whether the focus was on animals or humans, the message was that specific areas of the brain exerted control upon specific behavior.

As an illustration, for humans there is an area in the brain for speech recognition and another area for the recognition of music, and still a different area for writing; and yet another for speaking. The brain was gerry-mandered into regions for visual recognition, reading, touch, creating sentences — either written or spoken — and making music (Morgan and Stellar, 1950). Authors of those physiology textbooks referred to specific locations on the brain map as controversial among neurologists but a concept that is valuable for suggesting hypotheses for future research.

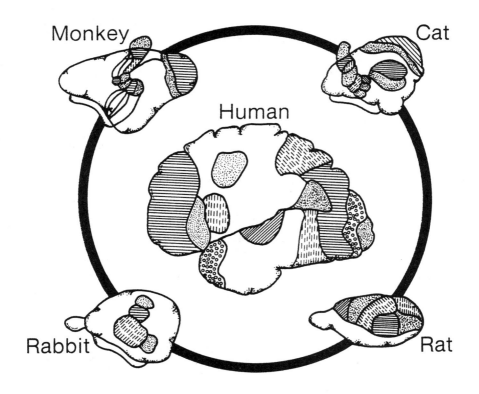

Figure 2

Even for animals, chapter-after-chapter divided the cerebral cortex into areas that were connected to specific behaviors. For example, the brain mapping showed different locations for arms, legs, face, vision, touch, hearing, and movement. Of course, the map makers were always tentative — always cautious in saying that a brain map of functions has yet to be firmly established.

Recently, for example, Rosenfield (1986) reported that brain maps not only vary from animal to animal, but over time, the brain map may change its boundaries within a single animal. Also, if there is neural damage, the boundaries of the brain map may change, presumably to "compensate" — or repair the defective area.

Sperry's Nobel-prize winning demonstration

The demonstration that won the Nobel Prize for Roger Sperry is marvelously simple. Of course, Professor Sperry worked in the laboratory for more than 30 years exploring the mysterious working of the brain before he created the key experiment. It was designed as follows: First, the two hemispheres of a cat's brain were separated. This was accomplished by cutting the corpus callosum which is a massive bundle of tissue that connected the right and left hemisphere in both animals and humans. (Incidentally, this is not a pain-inflicting surgical procedure for the animals since there are no pain-endings in the brain.)

The idea was to prepare the cat so that everything the animal sees with the right eye is flashed only to the right hemisphere and everything seen by the left eye travels only into the left hemisphere. The problem is this: Each point behind the right eye has a wire-like fiber that carries information from the eye back into the brain. Some of the fibers are connected directly in a straight line into the right hemisphere and some go kitty-corner into the left. Of course, the left eye works the same way.

It is a puzzling bit of anatomical architecture, but part of what we and animals see with our right eye is located on one side of the brain and part of the image is projected to the opposite side. Only half of each eye is wired to go straight back into the brain and the other half crosses over to the other hemisphere of the brain.

Those fibers going kitty-corner to the opposite hemisphere were cut at the location in the brain where they cross (called the optic chiasm), which means that an image registered by the right eye is seen only in the right hemisphere of the brain, and likewise, an image to the left eye was flashed only to the left brain.

Next, a black patch was placed over the cat's left eye so that what the animal saw with its right eye was projected only into the right hemisphere. Now the cat must solve a problem by seeing only with its right eye and right hemisphere of the brain. Visualize two swinging doors side by side. Behind one with a "V" painted on it there was food and behind the other with " Λ " there was nothing. Each time the hungry cat was released, it had to decide which door to nuzzle open for a reward of food. Of course, the door marked with a "V" that signaled food was varied randomly on each trial so that it could be on either the left or right each time the cat was released (Asher, 1981).

Results. As you would expect, the cat made many mistakes before it consistently, on every trial, walked directly to the door with a "V." The cat learned to make a discrimination and the learning was recorded in the right hemisphere of the brain only.

Now, what will happen if we reverse the patch to the right eye and also reverse the symbols on the doors so that the symbol " Λ " signals food hidden behind the door while "V" means no food? In cats that have *not* had the hemispheres of the brain divided, this task would be a difficult problem. We would expect *negative transfer* — that is, the normal cat would need **more trials** to learn the reversal than were needed in learning the original discrimination.

Here's what happened. The split-brain cats showed no negative transfer. The learning curve was almost identical for the reversal as for the original learning. It was as if the cat had never experienced the problem before. Literally, the left side of the brain did not know what the right had done. It was as if both sides of the brain learned the task independently.

APPLICATION TO PEOPLE

Surgeons had been following the basic laboratory research and noted that when the hemispheres were separated, the ordinary behavior of animals was not disrupted. The cats with a split-brain, for example, appeared to function quite normally. Therefore, they reasoned, this procedure may have practical applications for people who suffer from intractable pain resulting from convulsions. Since the seizures seem to originate in one hemisphere of the brain and spread like an electrical storm to the entire brain, if the corpus callosum was cut, then perhaps the convulsion could be localized to one hemisphere so that trauma would not radiate to the remainder of the brain.

The operation was remarkably successful — more than expected because in many cases, the seizures were not only reduced in magnitude, but eliminated. A by-product of this surgery was the opportunity to explore further the workings of the right and left hemispheres of the human brain because we now had people with both hemispheres of the brain divided. Although their ordinary everyday behavior appeared to be unaltered, on closer observation there were differences that were remarkable and quite controversial.

I have selected one case history to report to you, which I believe is representative of the general findings, but it is important to realize that there is variation from case to case and from study to study.

A case history. This is the case of P. S. as reported by Gazzaniga, Le Doux, and Wilson (1977). P. S. is a right-handed fifteen-year old boy who experienced severe epileptic attacks at about the age of two. He developed normally until the age of ten when the seizures started again and became intractable. In January 1976, the entire corpus callosum was surgically divided.

In one series of demonstrations after the operation, P.S. was seated a few feet from an opaque screen and instructed to fix his gaze on a dot in the center of the screen. Then a rear view projector flashed words or pictures on either the right or left side of the screen and P.S. was asked to tell what he saw. Here's what happened.

When the picture of an ordinary object, a key, was flashed on the right side of the screen, P.S. immediately said, "I saw a key." But when the object on the next trial

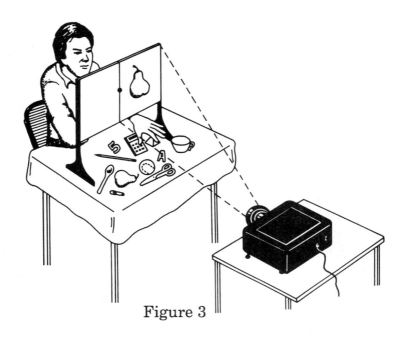

Figure 3

was an apple, which appeared for an instant on the left side of the screen, P.S. reported, "I didn't see anything." Curiously, P.S. correctly named all objects projected into the left brain (those appearing on the right side of the screen), but could not name any objects that were seen by the right hemisphere (those appearing on the left side of the screen). It was as if the right hemisphere was blind.

In the next demonstration, words for common objects such as a safety pin, tire, bicycle, and playing card were flashed on either side of the screen; again, a perfect score in naming items projected into the left hemisphere and "blindness" for items flashed into the right hemisphere.

The illusion of blindness. It seemed as if the right hemisphere of the brain was blind, but this was an illusion. The individual did see the pictures and the words projected into the right brain but he was not conscious of it — that is, he could not express the experience in words.

How do we know that? You will recall that the subject reported seeing nothing when, for instance, "apple" was flashed on the left side of the screen. But this time, the experimenters followed up with, "Please pick up a pencil with your left hand and write the word that just appeared on the screen." P.S. slowly scribbled the word "apple."

The researchers were astonished to discover that, even though P.S. reported seeing nothing for an item flashed to his right brain, he could *write, spell, point to,* or *pick up* the appropriate item with almost perfect accuracy.

They made the tests more complex. For example, P.S. was told, "When you see a word flashed on the screen, please say a word that is opposite. If, for instance, you see 'cat,' then you would say 'dog.' If you see 'girl,' you would say 'boy.'

The results. Again, "blindness" for words flashed to the right hemisphere, but on every trial he could point to the correct item from a set of four words. The same results were obtained when P.S. was asked, "This time when you see a word, give me a word that is associated. For instance, if you see 'clock,' you might say, 'time.' If the word is 'porch,' you might say 'house.'" When P.S. only had to point to an associate from among three choices, there was a perfect score by either the left or right hemisphere.

They tried this variation: "P.S., when you see a word,

tell me another word that rhymes. For instance, if you see 'canoe,' you would say 'new' or 'who.'" Again, if there were three choices to select from, P.S. had almost a perfect score for either hemisphere.

Clearly, the right hemisphere is mute — unable to talk — but it is processing information and can express itself if you provide a "voice box" such as *touching* objects, *pointing* to a choice from alternatives, or even *spelling*.

The right brain understood action verbs, because P.S. could point to a picture from a set of pictures that represented words such as "sleeping," "laughing," and "drinking." Remember, when each of those words appeared and were transmitted to the right hemisphere, P.S. reported, "I didn't see anything," yet he was able with almost perfect accuracy to point at the correct item in a set of choices.

The monitoring phenomenon. In ordinary everyday activity, messages are flickering back-and-forth at lightning-speed from one hemisphere to the other across the transmission circuits of the corpus callosum. But, the next demonstration with P.S. suggests something quite unusual. Not only are the right and left hemispheres capable of processing information independently, but each hemisphere may also be m*onitoring* the other.

The directions to P.S. were,"When you see a word such as 'laugh,' please laugh. If you see 'cry,' then cry." Then the command "rub" was flashed to the right hemisphere and the subject *rubbed* the back of his head with his left hand.

He was asked, "What was the command?"

He said, "itch."

It appeared as if a command was received in the right brain, followed by a change in behavior. The behavior was *observed* by the left hemisphere which made an interpretation. Notice that the left brain was not aware of what caused the movement in P.S. The left brain only observed P.S. lift his left hand to the back of his head and his fingers were moving on the back of the neck. The left brain guessed that P.S. was "itching his neck." It seemed reasonable just looking at what P.S. was doing.

The monitoring process was further shown in this demonstration: "P.S., assume the position of_____" and the word "boxer" was flashed to the right hemisphere. Immediately, P.S. shifted his body into a pugilistic stance.

"P.S., what word did you see?"

To the amazement of the researchers, P.S. answered without hesitation, "The word was boxer." Remember, in every previous test in which information, either words or pictures, was flashed to the right hemisphere, there was a response of, "I didn't see anything." Now, the right brain had suddenly found its tongue. It could speak and give an answer that was exactly on-target.

The demonstration was repeated, but just after "boxer" was projected to the right brain, P.S. was restrained from moving. Then he was asked, "What word did you see?"

He said, "I didn't see a word."

Moments later, when he was released, he assumed a pugilistic position and said, "OK, it was boxer."

Is each hemisphere of the brain monitoring the other? I believe this is a reasonable hypothesis. Notice, for example, what happened when the test was reversed with the left hemisphere receiving the commands. In the case of P.S., as an illustration, when a command such as "laugh" was flashed to the left hemisphere, the individual often uttered the word aloud, then executed the command. The utterance was heard by the right brain which then had the option of executing the instruction.

Incidentally, both hemispheres can recognize the correct response to a command when the person is only required to point to a picture in a set of pictures, but only the right hemisphere seems able to express appropriate behavior in response to commands.

SUMMARY

For several hundred years, the brain's landscape (for humans or animals) has been pictured as segmented for performing different functions. However, it was difficult for neuroanatomists to conceptualize each hemisphere of the brain as capable of a different function. Since both hemispheres appear to be almost identical to the naked eye, it seemed reasonable that they had an identical function. This hypothesis was even more convincing because other organs that are quite different in appearance, had identical functions such as the left-and-right lungs, the left-and-right kidneys, the left-and-right thyroid glands, and others.

Professor Roger Sperry of the California Institute of

Technology was the first to demonstrate with cats that each hemisphere of the brain (although they appear to be identical), can function independently. A blizzard of experiments by other researchers followed Dr. Sperry's work to show that not only can each hemisphere operate independently, but each seems to be sensitive to different input from the sensory receptors. Each brain seems to be decoding different messages. Not only is the decoding different, but the hemispheres are in communication with each other across the corpus callosum.

In the next chapter, I will present a picture of how the decoding seems to work for each hemisphere of the brain.

REFERENCES

Asher, J.J. The extinction of second language learning in American schools: An intervention model. In The *Comprehension Approach to Foreign Language Instruction* (H. Winitz, Ed.). Newbury House, Rowley, Massachusetts, 1981, 49-68.

Benson, D.F. Introduction. In *The Dual Brain* (D. F. Benson and E. Zaidel, Eds.). The Guilford Press, New York, 1985, 3-6.

Benson, D.F., and Zaidel, E.(Eds.) *The Dual Brain*. The Guilford Press, New York, 1985.

Gazzaniga, M.S. The split brain in man. *Scientific American,* 1967, 217(2), 24-29.

Gazzaniga, M.S., Le Doux, J.E., and Wilson, D. H. Language, praxis, and the right hemisphere: Clues to some mechanisms of consciousness. *Neurology,* 1977, 1144-1147.

Ghiselli, E.E. Mass action and equipotentiality of the cerebral cortex in brightness discrimination. *Journal of Comparative Psychology*, 1938, 25, 273-290.

Lashley, K.S. Factors limiting recovery after central nervous lesions. *Journal of Nervous Mental Disorders*, 1938, 88, 733-755.

Lober, J. Is your brain really necessary? *Science*, Vol. 210, 12, December 1980.

Lober, J. The disposable cortex. *Psychology Today*, 126, April 1981.

Lober, J. How much of a brain do you need? *Mind and Body*, 110, May 1981.

Maier, N.R.F. Cortical destruction in the posterior part of the brain and its effect on reasoning in rats. *Journal of Comparative Neurology*, 1932, 56, 179-214.

Morgan, C.T., and Stellar, E. *Physiological Psychology*. McGraw-Hill, New York, 1950.

Rosenfield, I. Neural Darwinism: A new approach to memory and perception. *The New York Review*, October 9, 1986.

CHAPTER 2

NEW CLUES TO EXPLAIN THE MYSTERY OF HYPNOSIS

A few years ago on an American television program, a nationally-known talk show host, Art Linkletter, said on the air to a person from the studio audience, "I'll give you five hundred dollars if you can tell me your name within thirty seconds."

The audience gasped. There is, of course, no information that we can recall more easily than our own name. After all, we have heard it more frequently in our lifetime than any other single item. Our own name is associated with a hundred thousand vivid and intimate experiences. What is more easily retrieved from our memory storage than our own name?

Immediately after Linkletter's question, the person uttered his name which was verified by showing a driver's license, and the host paid off with five new one-hundred dollar bills. What was the gimmick? Well, at that time Art Linkletter was exploring the topic of hypnosis which has intrigued almost every psychologist from Yale's famous Clark Hull to Stanford's Ernest Hilgard.

After the man from the studio audience slid the money into his wallet, he was led off-stage where a professional hypnotist worked with him for about twenty minutes. Then, the person reappeared on-stage and Linkletter said, "Now, I'll give you another five hundred dollars if you can tell me your name within thirty seconds."

The person hesitated, then replied, "It's on the tip of my tongue."

"Take your time," Linkletter calmly reassured the man, "I'll give you an additional thirty seconds."

"I knew it a few minutes ago, but I can't quite recall it."

What happened was that the hypnotist had given the man a post-hypnotic suggestion that when Art Linkletter asked for his name, he would not remember no matter how hard he tried. Notice that memory was dramatically altered without physical intervention — that is, without drugs and without surgery. Simply by talking to the person for a few minutes, the hypnotist produced a radical change in behavior.

Many psychologists who have investigated hypnosis in carefully controlled experiments are skeptical. Some have concluded that it is a fake because they believe that the person "under hypnosis" is play acting to please the hypnotist. Other psychologists have concluded that any so-called dramatic change in behavior observed while a person is in hypnosis can be produced while the person is normally functioning in everyday life. Hypnosis from this point of view, is a kind of self-suggestion which we exhibit frequently. For instance, many people can tell themselves when they go to bed that they will awaken at a certain time in the morning. They, in a sense, set themselves as a human alarm clock — and it seems to work with uncanny accuracy.

It is possible that self-suggestion is a talent which varies from person to person. It has been rather firmly established that there are vast individual differences in people's ability to be hypnotized (it seems to follow a normal curve), and there is variation from person to person in the depth of the hypnotic trance that each individual is able to attain. Generally, the greater the depth of the trance, the wider the array of behavior that can be elicited that is beyond the "normal limits" of human functioning.

For those who are excellent hypnotic subjects, extraordinary behavior has been observed over and over in thousands of demonstrations. For example, people can be told that they will temporarily be unable "to hear" and then a pistol is fired off unexpectedly near the subject's ear. Everyone in the room flinches reflexively except the subject. In medical situations, minor and even major surgery has been performed on people without chemical anesthesia. These people were hypnotized and told that they would experience "no feeling" in the part of the body that would be cut. Especially in medical applications of hypnosis such as major surgery, the faking hypothesis or the "I'm-doing-it-to-please-the-hypnotist" explanation is not very convincing.

What has been missing in the several hundred years that behavior under hypnosis has been observed is a persuasive explanation of what it is and why it seems to work. I believe that the recent breakthrough in brain research by Nobel Laureate Roger Sperry and his colleagues at the California Institute of Technology now provides us with a fresh insight into the nature of hypnosis.

The Brain. As you recall, the brain consists of two walnut-shaped hemispheres connected by a band of neural tissue called the corpus callosum. Sperry and his colleagues demonstrated that the corpus callosum is a kind of neural switchboard that transmits messages from one hemisphere to the other. When the neural switchboard is disconnected — this is done surgically by cutting the fibers of the corpus callosum — the right and left brain seem to operate independently.

For example, in a cat, if the neural wiring between the two hemispheres is cut, as was explained in Chapter 1, the animal can learn to solve a problem with one side of the brain only, without the awareness of the other half of the brain. The cat has a kind of double awareness in which each brain seems to think independently.

As a result of Sperry's work, surgeons reasoned that separating the right and left brain may relieve the severity of trauma in epileptic patients. Epileptic seizures often originate in one hemisphere of the brain and then radiate like an electrical storm to the other hemisphere. By cutting the corpus callosum, the massiveness of the seizure could perhaps be reduced. The operation worked.

A further discovery with these "split-brain" people is that the right and left brain (at least in right handed males from whom we have the most data) seem to operate quite differently. For example, when information goes into the left brain, such as a word or a picture, the individual can verbally report what he saw. If asked a question, the left brain can talk to explain what it has experienced.

If information goes into the right brain, however, and a question is asked such as, "What did you just see on the screen?" the person will say, "I didn't see anything." The right brain cannot communicate in words what it has experienced. Although the right brain cannot communicate in language, it can express itself if asked to *act out,* to *draw*, to *point*, to *spell*, to *sing*, or *physically demonstrate* with *body movements* such as *pantomime.*

Application of double awareness to hypnosis

My hypothesis is that hypnosis is a non-surgical procedure for disconnecting the neural switchboard that is wired to both halves of the brain, thereby producing a person with two independent brains. In hypnosis, the individual temporarily functions as a person with a "split-brain." The individual has a double consciousness. In hypnosis, I believe that brainswitching can be disconnected so that no messages are being transmitted from one hemisphere of the brain to the other.

Specifically, I am suggesting that the hypnotic trance short-circuits, in a sense, the left brain so that only the right brain is receiving information. For example, it is well established that the individual in hypnosis does not seem to be evaluating incoming information. Screening information for its believability seems to be the role of the left brain. The left hemisphere accepts only what is logical, reasonable, sensible, and realistic. It is comfortable with the familiar. It seems to operate to keep us "safe and sane." Hence, it is skeptical, critical, and cautious. It whispers to us, "Better to be safe than sorry," "Look before you leap," and "Stick to what you know." Often it will use ridicule and sarcasm to invalidate unfamiliar ideas.

The right brain operates according to rules that are still enigmatic, but one can glimpse how the right brain works from night dreams in which anything, no matter how bizarre, is possible and believable, until one awakes and the content of the dream is reviewed by the ever-skeptical left brain.

Color Blindness. In 1939, research psychologist, M. H. Erickson published in the *Journal of General Psychology* an article which one reviewer called "unquestionably one of the best studies of its kind, because it was so carefully done." Dr. Erickson did this: He hypnotized people and when they were in a trance, he told them, "You will not be able to see colors."

If brainswitching has been disconnected, then all tests will show the person to be color blind if the test requires the individual to respond with a *verbal answer* because the right brain is unable to express itself in language. But, if the person can somehow demonstrate physically (that is, act-out the answer), it will communicate that the person is *not* color blind.

Here is what happened. Erickson used the Ishihara test for color blindness which is a series of cards covered with different colored spots. If a person's color vision is normal, the individual will detect a number camouflaged in the dense array of colored spots on each card. If the person is totally color blind, the individual will report that no number was seen on any of the cards. Some people who are partially color blind will see some numbers and not others.

The results. Erickson's subjects **said** that they saw no numbers on any of the cards. Seemingly, hypnosis had produced total color blindness, But had it? If brainswitching is disconnected in hypnosis then when the right brain saw numbers on each of the Ishihara cards, it was unable to send a message across the corpus callosum to the left brain. Hence when Dr. Erickson asked each person what number they saw on each card, the answer would be, "I don't see a number."

However, even though brainswitching has been temporarily short-circuited, results should be entirely different if the right brain has a "voice box" to communicate that it did see the colors. For example, instead of showing the individual under hypnosis an Ishihara card and saying, "Now please tell me what you see," ask the person to reach with the left hand and pick up a number that was on the Ishihara card just shown.

My hypothesis predicts that the person should say, "I do not see a number," but with the left hand, the person will pick up the appropriate number. The problem, of course, with Dr. Erickson's 1939 experiment is that at that time, psychologists were unaware that how the subject responds is critical. At that time, the model of the brain was one of a unified entity functioning as a holistic unit. Hence, almost all experiments only required subjects to respond verbally either with a spoken answer or in writing.

Fortunately, psychologist P.L. Harriman of Bucknell University circa 1940 inadvertently performed an experiment which is a direct test of the brainswitching hypothesis. He told individuals who were in a deep hypnotic trance (incidentally, the depth of the trance is an important variable), that they would not be able to see the color red.

At this point he tested each person with the Homgren Color Test. It works like this: You present a sample of cloth that has a color such as *rose* and ask the individual to pick up other samples, from an assortment of colors, that match the rose. Next, present a sample of a red cloth which the subject is supposed to match by selecting reds from the assortment. Finally, the target is green and the person with normal vision should pick up other greens in the array.

Subjects in the deep trance were told by Dr. Harriman that they could not see red. What will happen when a rose cloth is placed in front of the subject with these instructions, "Here is a piece of cloth. Please select other fabrics from this assortment that match the cloth in front of you."

If a person is actually blind to red (this is called "propanopia"), here is what will happen: The individual will pick up different fabrics that match rose, and among the choices will be samples of blue. That is quite a dramatic mix up, but it is to be expected if an individual has some optical defect that produced genuine organic red-blindness.

The results. The hypnotized subjects (who were told that they could not see red) never picked up a blue sample and matched it with a rose. They confused rose with similar hues such as red and brown. Some occasionally confused rose with grey, but never did anyone select a blue patch as a match for rose. This suggests to me that when a verbal report is asked for, the left side of the brain answers with, "I do not see the color," but if the right hemisphere is asked to reach out a hand and grasp the target from an array, there is an accurate response. The left side of the brain was color blind but the right was not. Probably the right side saw the correct colors on each trial but was unable to communicate this information across the corpus callosum to the left hemisphere.

Dr. Harriman concluded that when people under heavy hypnosis are told that they are color blind for red or green, they truly cannot see either red or green. But — and here is the intriguing puzzle — although the hypnotized persons cannot see red or green, they do not react on tests as we would expect people to respond who have genuine color blindness of propanopia (red-blindness) or deuteranopia (green-blindness).

Conclusion. The right side of the brain was making accurate color discriminations but not transmitting any information to the left hemisphere that the left side did not want to know. This may be analogous to the "unhearing" responses when people are asked to "shadow" with the left ear — that is, listen only with the left ear.

For example, when utterances are spoken simultaneously into both ears through earphones, individuals are aware only of the utterances heard by the left ear. People can choose not to hear what was said to the right ear. This is sometimes referred to as the "cocktail party" phenomenon in which one is in a room filled with people talking but the person is able to focus only on one conversation and not hear what others are saying.

It would seem from the evidence that sensory data are coming into the receptors (i.e. eyes, ears), processed in the right hemisphere, but some of the messages are blocked before reaching the left hemisphere. Hence, the individual in hypnosis who has been instructed not to see red, does not experience red in the left hemisphere. In hypnosis, we have clues as to how brainswitching works.

Blindness. In 1935, the *British Journal of Medical Psychology* published the results of ingenious experiments in hypnosis by Frank A. Pattie, Jr. who was then a Professor of Psychology at Rice University in Houston,

Texas. One of Dr. Pattie's most responsive subject's was placed into a deep trance and told that she was blind in one eye. Then, she was directed to open her eyes and her vision was tested with the standard oculist's acuity chart. When she stood 20 feet away from the chart with only her "blind "eye open, she said, "I can see no letters on the chart."

"All right," said Professor Pattie, "move closer to the chart until you can see the letters."

She came within two feet of the chart, and said that she still could not read any of the letters on the chart.

When she was asked to put on a pair of colored spectacles, she could not tell what color was before the "blind" eye. If a hand was passed across her face and she was asked, "What do you see?" she would respond, "I saw a flicker or perhaps a momentary brightness."

"Try again. Do you recognize any object?" And Pattie passed his hand slowly in front of the "blind" eye.

"No."

She *said* that she could not read the letters on the eye chart, nor could she detect color, nor could she even see a hand in front of her face. Yet, when Dr. Pattie increased and decreased the intensity of light into her "blind" eye, the pupil expanded and contracted as if it were normal. When a light was flashed into the "blind" eye, the lids blinked normally. When a fist was feigned towards the "blind" eye, she reflexively moved her head backwards.

In 1935, faking seemed to be the most reasonable explanation because although the woman *said* that she could not see with the "blind" eye, the physical tests showed normal vision. But, the split-brain data fits the results with remarkable precision. For example, the right hemisphere read the letters on the eye chart, detected the change in color when she put on the special spectacles, and saw the hand that was passed in front of her face. But, the right brain could not transmit the messages to the left brain; therefore, the woman had a left brain experience of genuine blindness.

Notice that the woman was asked to give a talking response each time and talk is controlled by the left hemisphere. Only when non-talking responses, such as reflexes, were required did the right side communicate that it was not blind even though the left was. For example, when the brightness of light was increased and decreased into the "blind" eye, the right hemisphere communicated normal vision through the appropriate expansion and contraction of the pupil. When the experimenter made a fist and feigned a punch towards her "blind" eye, the right hemisphere showed that it could see the object coming and responded by averting the woman's head.

There was no malingering. There was no faking.

In an attempt to demonstrate conclusively that indeed she was faking, Dr. Pattie designed a follow-up study which was remarkably similar to "cross-cueing" studies conducted 30 years later with people who had their brain surgically divided. "Cross-cueing" works like this: A red light is flashed to the right brain and the person is asked, "What color was the light?" to which the person responded with, "I don't know."

"Please guess."

The left brain guesses by saying, "It was a green light." The right brain knew this was a mistake and communicated the error with a frown and shaking of the head. Amazingly, the left hemisphere noted the facial contortion and the person said, "Oh, I made a mistake. The color is red." This was called "cross-cueing."

Back to Dr. Pattie's hypnotic subject: The woman while in a trance was told that she was "blind" in one eye. Next, she was asked to look into a viewer (called a stereoscope) as different colors, one at a time, were presented to her "blind" eye. The individual angrily protested with, "This is absurd, Dr. Pattie. I cannot see any color."

"Please try. Even if you cannot see, guess what the color might be."

When 100 color changes were presented, the woman responded with 65 correct "guesses." After every guess, Professor Pattie responded with either "right" or "wrong."

The next day, the person was hypnotized again, the color test repeated, and the results were astonishing. In 100 trials, the person made only 2 mistakes. Can cross-cueing explain the results? I believe so. Here is my interpretation: The subject never made an immediate response when asked to name the color that was exposed to the "blind" eye. The response from the woman was delayed for about two seconds. Later, the person told Dr. Pattie that when color finally appeared, it was just a tiny flash.

However, believing that the woman was malingering, Professor Pattie interrogated her relentlessly.

Under hypnosis, he asked her, Were you aware of faking any tests?"

"No."

"Did you believe that your eye was actually blind?"

The woman was emphatic. "It was blind."

"These experiments show that your eye is not blind, don't they?"

"I suppose it isn't (blind) if you think so. But it is," she insisted. Then she added, " I will say that (the eye was not blind) if you want me to say it."

Then with the persistency of Agatha Christie's French detective, Dr. Pattie stepped the woman down into a deeper trance and continued to interrogate her to expose the "method of deception." He wrote later in his journal article that, "She clenched her fists, tossed about in the chair, and showed a great deal of agitation in her vocal and facial expressions." He interpreted this agitated behavior as resistance to telling the truth.

My interpretation is that the woman had told the truth, which the researcher would not accept. The pressure was on her to lie and to fabricate a justification for the lie. Clearly he wanted her to invent a technique of deception. Only this would satisfy him.

Well, she tried. It was acute stress for her. "She showed signs of great agitation and began to cry, " Pattie wrote in his report. She repeated many times, "I don't know. It is something I can't remember."

After more probing, she "confessed" and explained

how she had faked many of the tests. Only one of her explanations was verified; the others were, in my judgment, invented to please the interrogator. I believe this because Dr. Pattie said to her, "Are you ashamed to tell your methods of faking?"

She said, "No."

"Tell me, why did you show so much resistance in talking about your faking?"

"Because I can't remember."

Later he asked, "Do you feel humiliation in giving these reports?"

Enigmatically, she said, "Yes, something does, and something doesn't. I want to tell the truth, and I know it and something doesn't want to. Something makes me keep forgetting it, and I know it. It just goes, and I can't say it, and it makes my head ache and swim."

This is understandable. The right hemisphere knows that her eye was not blind, but her left hemisphere did not know it. The conflict is indeed understandable.

It is not inconceivable that we could have produced that similar emotional writhing in our split-brain patients if we had insisted that they could see what was coming into their right hemisphere, and accused them of lying when they said they saw nothing. If we assumed that they were faking and then relentlessly questioned them to detect their method of deception, the result is apt to be great agitation with clenched fists, tossing about and crying. They would probably insist that they didn't know and couldn't remember. And if we continued to persist, they may invent explanations to please us.

Since Professor Pattie's pioneer experiments were completed in 1935 — about 30 years before the split-brain operations, faking, at that time, seemed to be a reasonable explanation for the behavior observed.

Blind People Who Could See

It is like a riddle in a children's book: How can a person be blind and yet see? How can a person be deaf and yet hear? How can someone feel pain and not feel pain?

All of those contradictory and impossible behaviors were observed in the responses of people under hypnosis, and many scientific detectives attempted to solve the mystery. The techniques they invented to decipher the puzzle were elegant for their simplicity and ingenuity. But, as they probed deeper into the puzzle, it became maddeningly incomprehensible. Consider first the experiments of psychologists Helge Lundholm and Hans Lowenbach from Duke University.

While an individual to be hypnotized was awake and seated comfortably in a chair, sensors were taped to different parts of the head. The intent was to record electrical activity simultaneously. The sensors registered electrical activity coming from the frontal, the parietal, and the occipital regions of the brain, then transmitted the signals to pens that made a zigzag pattern on a strip of moving paper. These patterns are called electroencephalograms (brain waves).

When a person's eyes are closed, the pens glide into smooth loops, one after another, like the track of a roller coaster. This is the alpha wave. When the eyes are open, the alpha wave disappears and a sharp angular up and down line is etched out continuously along the strip of moving paper. Even when a person's eyes are closed, the alpha wave will vanish if the individual hears a noise such as whistling or someone talking.

So, the electrical brain activity to be expected in a normal waking state is alpha when the eyes are closed, but the alpha wave will vanish if the individual hears a sudden noise or when the person's eyes open.

Next, Professor Lundholm directed the individual into a deep trance with these instructions: "Sleep, deeply and quietly . . . deeper . . . I will count to five and as I count you go into a deeper and deeper sleep. One, two, three, four, five . . ." Then he said, "I am going to wake you up. As you open your eyes you will find that this room is completely dark. You will not be able to see anything whatsoever. It will remain dark until I snap my fingers. Then it will be light again. I will count to three and on three you wake up. One, two, three."

When Lundholm flashed a light into the person's eyes, the eyes did not turn away, nor did the eyelids blink which would be expected from someone who was blind. The individual indeed seemed to be blind, except for this: When the light was flashed into the person's eyes, the pupils contracted as would be expected from someone who was sighted. An interesting contradiction, which was further complicated by the alpha waves which flowed endlessly in graceful loops when the "blind" person's eyes were closed, but disappeared when there was a sudden noise or the eyes were open.

The contradiction can be explained with

brainswitching. The right side of the brain which probably directs the autonomic nervous system could see as shown by the instrumentation. For example, there were reflexive responses such as the pupillary contractions when a bright light was flashed in the eyes and the pens oscillating up and down on the strip of moving paper recorded electrical brain activity. However, the experience of sight was not transmitted across the corpus callosum to the left hemisphere. Hence, the individual believed he could not see and would report sightlessness if asked for a verbal report.

Since eye movement and eyelid blinking are under voluntary control, the left hemisphere could direct these superficial reactions to be consistent with a belief of blindness.

Researchers Lundholm and Lowenbach concluded that "in none of the experiments did we ever obtain different or even questionable results" (p.148). Suggested blindness under hypnosis does not influence normal alpha rhythm.

Deaf People Who Could Hear

Lundholm and Lowenbach extended their experiments to suggestions that the individual would be deaf while in a deep trance. Once the person was in a hypnotic "sleep," Lundholm said, "In a little while I shall say, '*now.*' From that moment on, you will be unable to hear any sound or voice except my own voice. This condition will last until I say '*now*' a second time. Then you will be able to hear. Now . . ."

At this point, Lowenbach who was outside the room gave a shrill whistle, called out in a loud voice to the individual and asked the person to solve simple mathematical problems. Inside the room, Lundholm observed that the individual made "no response of any kind" to the auditory stimulation. Each individual who participated in the experiment seemed to be temporarily deaf.

If there was genuine deafness, the alpha readings should be uninterrupted when there were whistles and voices, but just as we would expect from hearing people, the alpha waves immediately disappeared suggesting that there was normal hearing. Again the conflict: Individuals seemed to be deaf, yet the physiological signals showed no deafness. My hypothesis is that the right hemisphere which monitors the autonomic nervous system did hear the whistles and voices, but the information was not transmitted across the corpus callosum to the left hemisphere.

To Be in Pain and Not Be in Pain

A person is placed in a deep hypnotic "sleep" and told, "Now you have lost all feeling in your left arm. If something touches it, you won't be able to feel it at all."

A needle is stuck through the skin of the person's left arm.

The individual does not flinch and the facial expression does not change. The hypnotist asks, "Did you feel anything?"

The answer is, "No."

Psychologist M. Levine did this exact experiment at Johns Hopkins Hospital in 1930. Since then, the demonstration has been repeated thousands of times.

The question is: The person did not seem to experience any pain, but is this an illusion? With the proper suggestion in a normal waking state, would a person also feel no pain from, for instance, a needle?

There are great individual differences in tolerance for pain, but as with blindness and deafness, pain in hypnosis has a mystery. It is this: If people are put into a deep hypnotic sleep, and it is suggested that they have "no feeling" in parts of the body, they seem to experience no pain. The absence of pain is so real that surgical amputations and oral surgery have been performed on people who were under hypnosis.

But, even though the patients don't flinch or scream or cry, are they still experiencing pain? Strangely, that is exactly what the evidence suggests. For example, at Harvard University's Laboratory of Social Relations, psychologist Ronald E. Shor created the following experiment. Everyone participating in Dr. Shor's experiment was given "an extremely painful electric shock." There were five different situations.

In one situation, people were normally awake when they received the shock. In another situation, people were awake, but instructed to block out voluntarily any physiological reactions to pain such as flinching or facial grimace. In the third situation, people were hypnotized but given no suggestions that they would not experience pain. In the fourth, people were hypnotized and told voluntarily to block out physical reactions to pain. And finally, a group of people were hypnotized and told that they would have no feeling in a limb.

What happened? For all subjects, the automatic physical indicators showed that everyone including those in hypnosis had reacted when they got the electric shock. For example, for all subjects, sensors on the skin recorded an average of 1000 ohm shift in the reading when the electric shock was administered, and for all subjects there was a 5 beat per minute change in heart rate.

Outwardly, people who were awake were able to look calm, but they said that the shock was "very painful." Now, here is the mystery — the hypnotized group who were told that they would lose feeling in a limb, *said that they did not experience the shock as painful.*

Brainswitching fits these data also. The right hemisphere, I believe, did experience the pain from the electric shock and communicated this in the changes in the ohms reading and heart rate. But, the pain signal was not shunted into the left hemisphere for those who were hypnotized. Hence, when the hypnotized were asked whether they had experienced pain, they said no.

Further Clarification: Recent Evidence

Professor Ernest Hilgard of Stanford University has published in 1987 a book entitled, *Divided Consciousness* which further increases our understanding of the unusual behavior people experience under hypnosis.

Hilgard and his co-workers demonstrated that everyone is not equally able to experience hypnosis. Some people are more hypnotizable than others. For people who have a high ability to be hypnotized, when they are in a normal waking state, they are more responsive to suggestions that they will *not* feel pain or they will *not* hear tones presented at different intensities.

As an example, for people who were high in their ability to be hypnotized, 93% experienced some reduction in pain when their hand and forearm was immersed in circulating ice water for 45 seconds. In comparison, for those low in their ability to be hypnotized, only 44% experienced a reduction in pain.

The data for hearing reduction were similar to pain reduction. For those who were high in hypnotizability, 56% experienced some reduction in hearing the tones while only 9% of those low in hypnotizability had a hearing loss for tones.

It may be that the more able one is to experience hypnosis, the more control one has in screening the blocking signals traveling from one side of the brain to the other across the corpus callosum. This control may be possible even in a normal waking state since those high in hypnotizability seem to have a well-developed creative imagination. For example, they are adept at picturing in their imagination a storefront across the street and then in their fantasy, walk closer and closer to inspect in vivid detail items in the store window. This suggests an ease of access between the hemispheres which may be related to creative thinking by these individuals. This talent, incidentally, may be important for writers of fiction.

The Hidden Observer

My hypothesis is that one side of the brain — the "quiet" side — did experience pain, hearing, and sight but was unable in hypnosis to transmit the information across the corpus callosum to the "talkative" side of the brain. Hence, people under hypnosis say they did not feel pain or hear voices and whistles or see light flashed in their eyes. Professor Hilgard has developed evidence to support this idea. He uses the metaphor of a "hidden observer" to characterize that part of the cerebral system that experiences and knows information denied to another part of the system.

For example, a university student was hypnotized by the instructor and told that at the count of three, he would be completely deaf to all sounds, but his hearing would be restored to normal when the instructor's hand was placed on the student's right shoulder. Then to demonstrate that the student would not hear, large wooden blocks were banged close to his head. There was no flinching reaction, not even when a starter's pistol was fired repeatedly near his ear.

Then the instructor said in a quiet voice:

> As you know, there are parts of our nervous system that carry on activities that occur out of awareness, of which control of the circulation of the blood, or the digestive processes, are the most familiar. However, there may be intellectual processes also of which we are unaware, such as those that find expression in night dreams. Although you are hypnotically deaf, perhaps there is one part of you that is hearing my voice and processing the information. If there is, I should like the index finger of your right hand to rise as a sign that this is the case.

To the surprise of all in the room, the finger rose.

In an attempt to communicate with the *hidden observer,* the instructor suggested that when he placed a hand on the student's arm. "... I can be in touch with

. . . that part of you that could hear and know what was going on when you were hypnotically deaf."

Then the individual was awakened from the hypnotic trance and when questioned, could not recall any details about the experience. However, when the instructor placed his hand on the person's arm, immediately the individual could describe exactly what the instructor had said, that wooden blocks had been banged together and a pistol was fired repeatedly.

The Hidden Observer of Pain

In ten years of research by Hilgard and his coworkers, when people were instructed under hypnosis that they feel no pain, they reported an absence of pain when a hand and forearm were placed in circulating ice water or a tourniquet was fastened tightly to the upper arm. When the individuals were awakened from the trance, there was "never a single report of the memory of pain returning spontaneously . . ." (p.188).

Apparently, pain had been successfully eliminated while people were in hypnosis. But, is it possible that the "hidden observer" — the "quiet" side of the brain had indeed experienced the intensity of the pain but was unable to communicate with the left side?

To find out, Hilgard did this: After people were hypnotized, they were told that they would have no feeling in their right hand and arm that was then immersed in ice water. The hypnotist said, "Please keep your hand in the water until I ask you to remove it. Now, zero means no pain and ten means the pain is so severe, you want to remove it from the water. Start with zero and begin counting if the pain increases."

In a waking condition, people reached ten or above in *less than one minute.* But while they were in hypnosis, they continually responded with "zero" when asked at five second intervals about the experience of pain.

The twist is this. With the right hand in the ice water, the hypnotist instructed the "hidden observer" to communicate the experience of pain through the left hand by writing a number starting with zero for no feeling of pain.

What happened is that while the person verbally said "zero, zero, zero . . ." indicating no experience of pain, the left hand was simultaneously writing 1,2,3,4,5, . . . indicating a normal experience of pain.

As a qualifier, it should be pointed out that this dramatic demonstration was shown for people who had a high ability to be hypnotized.

Selective Perception

Experiments in psychology have established rather firmly that we respond to only a small portion of the sensory data that flood into our senses continually by the billions. This is called *selective perception.* I believe there is a gating mechanism between the right and left hemispheres that regulates this selective perception. In hypnosis, and in the split-brain studies, we glimpse clues as to how the gating works.

It looks as if all of the sensory information is received into the right hemisphere where a decision is made about which signals will be transmitted to the left hemisphere of our "awareness." Somehow, in hypnosis the decision-making process can be distinctly influenced. It can be altered. In hypnosis, we can intervene to tinker directly with the gating mechanism that shunts information from the right to the left hemisphere.

I believe the clearest evidence of gating can be seen when the hypnotized subject is asked to *physically act* rather than merely talk. Action by the individual gives a "voice box" to the mute right hemisphere. If the subject is asked to respond with talk, the communication is only with the left hemisphere. When the individual is asked to act, the right hemisphere has a chance to express itself.

A dramatic illustration of this is a study by Helge Lundholm of Duke University. In the autumn of 1939, he placed a cigar, a pencil and watch on a table in front of an excellent hypnotic subject. The woman was hypnotized and instructed that when she awoke, the cigar "would no longer be on the table." Of course, the cigar was never removed from the table.

Now, if the woman is asked whether there is a cigar on the table, the left hemisphere should answer that it does not see the object on the table. And, that is exactly what the woman said. But what does the right hemisphere see? It should see the cigar on the table but does not have the "voice box" to communicate what it sees.

However, a "voice box" can be created by asking the woman to "point to the place where the cigar used to be." When Dr. Lundholm did this, he reported in the journal titled, *Character and Personality,* that "She made a rapid sweeping movement with her arm, a movement that at one cross-section of its course brought her pointing finger to a place about three inches distant from the cigar." Then, while the woman was still under hypnosis, he suggested to her that when she was awake, she would recall fully the experiment.

Later, the conversation went like this:

"What do you remember?" he asked her.

"You told me that I could not see the cigar."

"And could you?"

"No, I could not see it. I honestly believed that it was not there."

"What happened when I asked you to point to where the cigar used to be?"

"When I pointed . . . I thought that I nearly saw it."

It is interesting that the right hemisphere for an instant, almost had a breakthrough to the left hemisphere.

The absence of interplay between the left and right brain would account for a network of puzzling behaviors observed while people are in hypnosis. For example, an individual under deep hypnosis was told that when he was awakened he will not see the table.

The person remarked later, "What happened to the table? Did someone take it away when I was in the trance?" However, even though the person comments that the table is absent, the individual will walk around the table and not collide into it.

Can Hypnosis Improve Our Skills?

For vision, audition, and pain, the evidence seems to

support the double consciousness hypothesis which is that one-half of the brain — the left hemisphere can be "blind," can be "deaf," and not aware of pain, but simultaneously, the right brain may have normal vision and normal audition and be acutely aware of pain. But can hypnosis *improve* a person's vision, hearing, or any other sensory function? Dr. Andre M. Weitzenhoffer of Stanford University reviewed the evidence in his book, *Hypnotism*, and concluded that hypnosis *cannot* improve any of our normal sensory functions.

If sensory functions cannot be improved, how about *memory* or *physical skills* such as playing golf or tennis? Perhaps the most thorough exploration to find the answers to self-improvement through hypnosis was conducted in a series of carefully controlled experiments by Paul Campbell Young. This research was Professor Young's doctoral dissertation at Harvard and was published in the *American Journal of Psychology*.

The question was: Under hypnosis can performance for simple skills be improved such as the strength of hand grip, the steadiness of the hand in tracing a pattern, and the sensitivity of skin to touch? Can a person increase the speed in being able to spell backwards or saying the alphabet backwards? Can simple memory for numbers and symbols be improved? How about improving the speed and accuracy for adding a column of numbers?

When Dr. Young compared the performance of people under hypnosis with those who were not hypnotized, the groups were about equal in skill. Dr. Young's results have increased credibility when you consider that he compared each person who was hypnotized with their performance when they were not hypnotized. The results showed that individuals could not out-perform themselves under hypnosis.

Other researchers such as Professor H. S. Eysenck from the University of London followed up the Young study and found some evidence for improvement under hypnosis for two excellent subjects who were capable of submerging into a deep trance. Professor Eysenck said in the *British Journal of Medical Psychology* that the most dramatic improvements were demonstrated for simple tests such as matching the length of lines, saying whether colors were the same or different, the precision movement of an arm, putting a dot accurately in circles that were moving past on a strip of paper and adding (or subtracting) numbers. No improvement was seen for more complex skills such as short-term memory for symbols or numbers, giving an accurate estimation of the number of dots on a card that is briefly seen, or detecting tiny changes in loudness or pitch.

Any improvement in skills that are observed while a person is in hypnosis may simply be the result of "quieting" the critical left brain which then allows the person to relax and give an optimal performance. To explore this idea further, I recently asked college students anonymously to rate themselves on a 10 point scale for how critical they are of others and of themselves. The results showed that students were significantly more critical of themselves with an average self-rating of about 7 compared with an average rating of 5 for how critical they were of other people.

If people tend to be highly self-critical, this may impair their performance on any skill. Under hypnosis, if the source of that critical behavior has been quieted, then the performance may naturally improve. Hypnosis may release the inhibitions that are created by the left brain.

Incidentally, the short-circuiting of brainswitching under hypnosis explains, I believe, the dramatic change in memory of the person from Art Linkletter's studio audience. When Linkletter asked the man to say his name, the left brain was unable to receive information across the corpus callosum from the right brain. The individual could have given a correct response if the right brain had been permitted to "answer" by pressing letters to spell his name or pointing to it from among other printed names or perhaps even singing. The right brain knew the correct response but was mute.

Further research in brain lateralization and hypnosis may open up new ways that we can achieve skill in quieting what may be our greatest adversary — the left brain and communicating more directly with the right brain. Problem solving skills can be enhanced as we gain voluntary control of the signals that flicker back-and-forth from one hemisphere to the other across the corpus callosum. More and more access to the "quiet" side of the brain may mean that we increase the chances for successfully coping with problems by discovering and creating more options.

Sigmund Freud's concept of a "conscious" and an "unconscious" mind was a brilliant approximation that should now be modified. Both minds seem to be conscious, but one can talk about its experience while the other cannot. And, if the "quiet" brain is given a way to communicate, it can transmit a stream of messages which may be vital to our well-being.

SUMMARY

Hypnosis temporarily permits the short-circuiting of brainswitching so that messages are blocked from being transmitted across the corpus callosum from one side of the brain to the other. The preponderance of the evidence from experimentsconducted in the past 75 years seems to support the hypothesis that under hypnosis, behavior is observed that matches the split-brain patients. There is, in other words, a state of double awareness in which the left and right brain operate independently with an absence of inter-hemispheric communication.

Since hypnosis is a non-chemical and non-surgical event involving only the focusing of attention to achieve an "altered state," the implication is that as our understanding of brainswitching increases, we will be able voluntarily to control the flow of communication from one hemisphere to the other. If we can direct the neural transmission of messages, we have the potential for enhanced problem solving by creating and discovering more options. Voluntary control of inter-hemispheric messages may also be the key to the assimilation of information on the first exposure.

REFERENCES

Dorcus, R. M. Modification by suggestion of some vestibular and visual responses. *American Journal of Psychology,* 1937, *49,* 82-87.

Erickson, M.H. The induction of color blindness by a technique of hypnotic suggestion. *The Journal of General Psychology,* 1939, *20,*

Erickson, M. H. & Erickson, E. M. The hypnotic induction of hallucinatory color vision followed by pseudo negative after-images. *Journal of Experimental Psychology,* 1938, *22,* 581-588.

Eysenck, H. J. An experimental study of the improvement of mental and physical functions in the hypnotic state. *British Journal of Medical Psychology,* 1941, *18,* 304-316.

Harriman, P. L. Hypnotic induction of color vision anomalies: I. The use of the Ishihara and the Jensen tests to verify the acceptance of suggested color blindness. *Journal of General Psychology,* 1942, *26,* 289-298.

Harriman, P.L. Hypnotic induction of color vision anomalies: II. Results on two other tests of color blindness. *Journal of General Psychology,* 1942, *27,* 81-92.

Hilgard, E. R. Hypnosis. *Annual Review of Psychology,* 1965, *16,* 157-180.

Hilgard, E. R. Hypnosis. *Annual Review of Psychology,* 1975, *26,* 19-44.

Hilgard, E. R. *Divided Consciousness.* New York: John Wiley & Sons, 1987.

Levine, M. Psychogalvanic reaction to painful stimuli in hypnotic and hysterical anesthesia. *Bulletin Johns Hopkins Hospital,* 1930, *46,* 331-339.

Lundholm, H. A new laboratory neurosis. *Character and Personality,* 1940, *9,* 111-121.

Lundholm, H., & Lowenbach, H. Hypnosis and the alpha activity of the electroencephalogram. *Character and Personality,* 1942, *11*, 145-149.

Pattie, F. A. A report of attempts to produce uniocular blindness by hypnotic suggestion. *British Journal of Medical Psychology,* 1935, *15*, 230-241.

Shor, R. E. Explorations in hypnosis: A theoretical and experimental study. Unpublished doctoral dissertation, Brandeis University, 1959.

Weitzenhoffer, A. M. *Hypnotism.* New York: Wiley & Sons, 1963.

Young, P. C. An experimental study of mental and physical functions in the normal and hypnotic states. *American Journal of Psychology,* 1925, *36*, 214-232.

CHAPTER 3

ILLUSIONS

INSIGHT INTO THE LOGIC OF THE LEFT BRAIN

Hypnosis may be a special case of visual illusions that have fascinated psychologists for more than a hundred years. For example, at Princeton University there is a room which is ordinary in appearance, but the floor and the walls have been constructed to produce the following illusion: An adult woman and a child walk into the room and stand in opposite corners against the far wall. The adult looks to be the size of a midget and the child appears to be a towering giant.

As you watch, the woman and the child turn and exchange places in the room so that each is now standing where the other was previously. Instantly, before your eyes, the size of the child shrinks from a giant to a midget and the woman expands, as she walks from one side of the room to the other, from a midget to a giant. This is the famous Ames illusion.

Amazingly, even after you are permitted to inspect the room from a different angle so that you see the distortions, when you return to your initial location, you see the room as "normal" and ordinary, but people dramatically change their physical size before your eyes as they move from one side of the room to the other.

What is so disconcerting about the Ames illusion is that "reality" vanishes instantly. After all, we have stored a hundred thousand experiences that validate a belief that when a person walks a few feet from us from one side of the room to the other, they do not suddenly expand and contract in physical size. Also, children usually are smaller in stature compared with adults.

I believe that illusions give us exciting clues about how messages are flashed from one hemisphere to the other — a process which I call brainswitching. For instance, in the Ames illusion, as you look at the scene, the room has been built so that it appears that the child and the adult are standing parallel to each other at equal distances from the observer. Actually, the person on the right (because of the trick construction of the room) is closer to the viewer than the person on the left. Hence, the retinal image of the person on the right (that is, the picture on the inside of the eye) will be larger than the retinal image of the person on the left.

This information, I believe, is evaluated at lightning-speed by the left brain as follows: First, we have the belief that both people are at *equal distances* from us — standing side by side at different corners of the room. If so, then the child should project a retinal image that is smaller compared with the adult. Actually, the retinal images do not match expectation based on distance. The retinal image of the child is huge compared with the adult (because the child is standing closer to us); hence we see the child as a giant and the adult as a dwarf.

When the two individuals turn and walk past each other, the adult is now standing closer to us physically while the child is farther away, but we continue to view them (because of the trick room) as standing at equal distances from us. If they are actually at equal distances, then the retinal image of the adult will be larger than the child, but the actual retinal images are that the the adult's picture on the inside of the eye is dramatically expanded while the child's picture is smaller than expectation.

What is intriguing about the Ames illusion is that we know and we firmly believe that young children are smaller in stature compared with adults. Even when we are permitted to examine the room and see that it has a trick construction in which the room is not a symmetrical rectangle, we continue to see the illusion when we view the scene again from an aperture in the wall. We experience a physical "impossibility" in which people we are watching dramatically change from dwarfs to giants and back to dwarfs. Apparently, our firmest beliefs about "reality" — those that we know are true based upon 100,000 valid experiences, can be reversed instantly.

Why do we see an illusion?

First, it appears that the adult and the child are at *equal distances* from the viewer. But actually, the child is *closer* to the viewer while the adult is *farther* away. Hence the image on the retina which is the back of the eye) is huge for the child and tiny for the adult. The left brain then interprets this fact to mean that the child must be giant while the adult is a midget.

In explaining this phenomenon, I am making the assumption that *depth perception** may be built into the human species at birth.

The evidence to support that depth perception may be innate is the "invisible cliff" phenomenon which works like this: A thick rectangle of glass is placed on top of a wooden table so that the glass extends beyond the

*We can fool the brain into believing that a two-dimensional scene is three-dimensional by letting each eye see the scene from a slightly different perspective as was the principle of the stereoscope which was a popular toy in the 1900s.

edges of the table. When an infant is then placed at the center of the table, the child will crawl to the edge of the table and not venture beyond which suggests that the infant is innately aware of depth. If so, then perhaps we project a "depth" interpretation on any two-dimensional surface. I will use this idea to explain why the brain creates many of the illusions you will see next.

I will present a selection of the famous visual illusions to illustrate the logic of the left brain that I believe operates as messages flicker back and forth between the right and left hemispheres of the brain at lightning-speed. Again, an assumption I am making is that *depth perception may be built into the human species at birth.*

Please look at the two lines presented below in Figure 4. Notice that the lines appear to be equal in length and if you measure the lines with a ruler, you will discover that they are, indeed, equal in length.

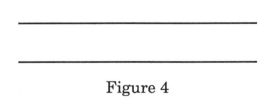

Figure 4

Nothing extraordinary about that until you add arrow heads to each line as you will see next in Figure 5. Now, suddenly, one horizontal line appears to be shorter compared with the other line — but they are still identical in length. If you don't believe it, use a ruler to measure the lines. What you are looking at in Figure 5 is the famous Müller-Lyer illusion.

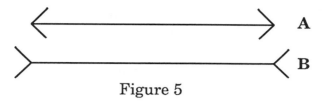

Figure 5

The horizontal lines in A and B are equal, but we see the line in A as shorter than the line in B. The logic of the brain may be as follows: The total figure in A is *smaller* compared with the total figure in B. Why?

There are only three components in each figure that could explain why the figure in A is *smaller* than the figure in B. The first is the angles made by the endings of the figures, but these appear to be equal. The second is the cosines that the angles make with the horizontal lines, but these appear to be equal.

The only remaining component is the horizontal lines. If figure A is smaller than figure B, *it must be* because the horizontal line in A is *shorter* compared with the horizontal line in B. This conclusion from the left brain's evaluation of the visual image is what we "see."

Notice that the illusion disappears immediately in Figure 6 when we add two lines that make the total figure in A equal to the total figure in B.

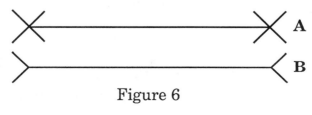

Figure 6

Next, in Figure 7 is a variation of the Müller-Lyer illusion in which, again, the horizontal lines in A and B are *actually equal,* but we tend to see the line in A as longer compared with the line in B.

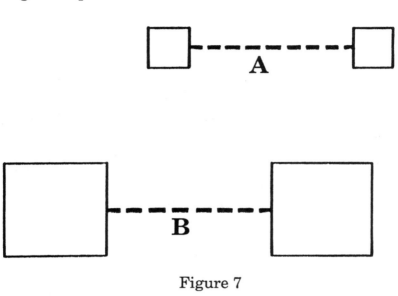

Figure 7

The left brain's logic for Figure 7 is this: Both entities appear to be *identical* except that A is farther away from us while B is closer (because we project "depth" into a two-dimensional scene).

If A is far and B is close, then on our retina, the horizontal dashed line in A should be *shorter* than the horizontal dashed line of B. Since this is not true, then actually (in the external world) the line of A is *not equal* to the line of B.

If A is far and B is close and the horizontal dashed line of A is actually *shorter* than the line of B, then the retinal image of A should have a shorter line compared with B. Since this is not true, A's horizontal line is not actually shorter than line B.

Finally, if A's horizontal line is not actually equal to or shorter than B, then the only other possibility is that the A line is *longer* than the B line which is the visual experience we call an illusion.

Figure 8 which you will see next, illustrates again the powerful input that "depth" has in the logical analysis the brain seems to make in creating visual experiences.

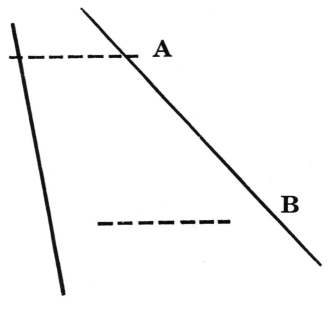

Figure 8

On the retina, lines that are actually parallel in the external world will *appear* to converge in the distance and that is exactly what the retina sees in Figure 8.

Hence, the conclusion is that horizontal line A is farther away than horizontal line B. If A is distant and B is closer and they are, in fact, identical in length, then on the retina, A should be shorter than B. Since the retinal image of A is not shorter than B, A is not *actually* equal to B in length.

The left brain concludes that, if A is actually shorter than B, and A is farther away than B, then on the retina, A should be shorter in length. Since this is not the case, then line A is not *actually* shorter compared with line B.

Therefore, if line A is not actually equal to or shorter than line B, the only remaining possibility is that line A is *actually* longer than line B and that cerebral conclusion is what we experience.

In Figure 9, the dotted lines in A are, by physical measurement, equal to the the dotted line in B; yet, the A line appears to be shorter compared with line B. Why?

The brain may reason as follows: First, the *total figure* in A is *smaller* than the *total figure* in B. What accounts for this fact? Since the circles for A appear on the retina to be equal to the circles in B, the figures are not at different distances.

Hence, if the difference in total size is not due to the size of the circles nor a difference in distance, the only remaining element is the horizontal line in each figure. Horizontal line A must be shor*ter* than horizontal line B and this is the illusion that we experience.

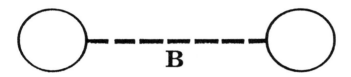

Figure 9

By physical measurement, the height of A, B, and C in Figure 10 are equal. Yet we "see" A as shorter than B and B as shorter than C. Why?

The left brain's logic may proceed as follows: First, A is closer to us than B and B is closer to us than C. Secondly, the pattern of all three appear on the retina to be identical. However, (a) if A, B, and C are *actually* identical in all properties including height and (b) if A is closer to the observer than B and B is closer than C, then, on the retina, A should be taller than B and B should be taller than C.

However, on the retina, A is not taller than B and B is not taller than C. The cerebral conclusion is that A, B, and C are not of equal height.

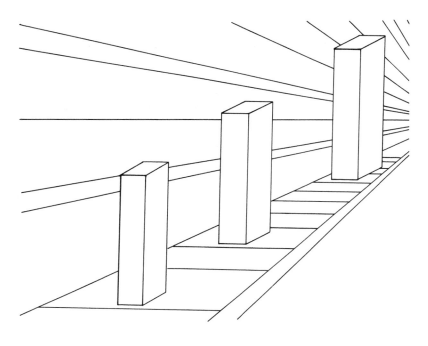

Figure 10

Next, if A is actually taller than B and B taller than C, then, on the retina, A should be taller than B and B should be taller than C. Since this condition is not met, A is not *actually* taller than B and B is not *actually* taller than C.

Notice that the left brain has eliminated two of three possibilities. For example, the brain has concluded that A=B=C is false and that A > B > C is also false. The only other possibility is that A < B < C (that is, A is shorter than B and B is shorter than C) which is our visual experience that we recognize as an illusion.

The left brain is *logically evaluating* incoming sensory data at lightning-speed and the end result is what we "see," what we "hear,"and what we "feel."

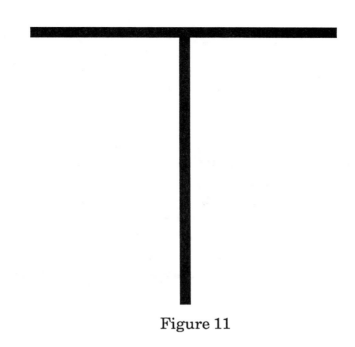

Figure 11

Figure 11 is the famous "top hat" illusion. Amazingly, if you put a ruler on the vertical and the horizontal lines, you will find that they are equal in length.

Simply, the crucial axiom here is that the upper half of vertical lines will appear to be shorter than they actually are. This has been demonstrated by Ladd-Franklin in which the upper half of a vertical line presented by itself seemed slightly longer to observers compared with the lower half of the vertical line. Apparently, the left brain evaluates a vertical line in three dimensions so that the upper half of the line is interpreted as receding in the distance.

The left brain's logic may be this: The vertical line signal's distance while the horizontal line does not. As the vertical line goes up, it moves farther away from us.

Hence, if the vertical (V) and horizontal (H) are actually equal in length, then, *on the retina,* V should be shorter than H. Since this is not the case, the brain concludes that V = H is false.

Next, if the vertical in the external world is actually shorter than the horizontal, then, *on the retina,* it should be shorter in length. Since this is not the case, the brain concludes that the interpretation of V being shorter than H is false. Again, the brain has eliminated two of three possibilities, namely that V is not equal to H and V is not shorter than H. This leaves only the possibility that actually, the vertical line is *longer* compared with the horizontal line and that is what we experience as the "top hat" illusion.

Figure 12

When "S" and "8" are presented in Figure 12 as we normally view them in reading, the upper and bottom halves of the figures appear about equal with the upper halves being seen perhaps as slightly smaller than the lower halves. However, if you invert the "S" and the "8" (as you see in Figure 13), why do the tops immediately appear distinctly larger than the bottoms?

The inversion of the familiar "S" and "8" as seen in

Figure 13, is a variation of the "top hat" illusion. The left brain seems to reason it out like this: If the upper part of a line or a figure is shorter on the retina compared with the bottom, then the *actual* line or figure has "a" equal to "b" or "a" is shorter than "b." Remember that distance is projected upon a two-dimensional figure with the upper part of a vertical line seen as receding in the distance.

Hence, if a =b is false and a < b is also false, then the only remaining possibility is that "a" is *larger* than b which is the illusion in Figure 13.

Figure 13

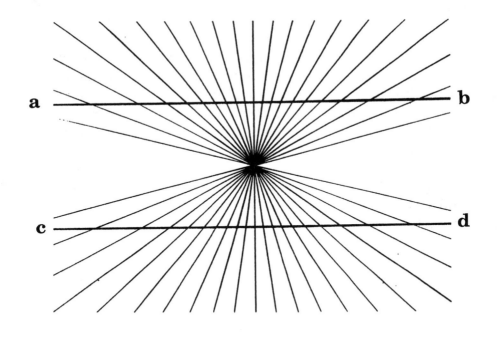

Figure 14

In Figure 14, the horizontal lines are parallel by physical measurement. Why is it that we see the top line curve concavely upward in the center and the bottom line curve concavely downward at its center?

If we view the figure as a two-dimensional configuration (which we do not), then each point on ab or cd will be observed to fall at an equal position on each triangle. In other words, every point of each horizontal line will fall at an equal altitude on each triangular section and we should see ab as parallel to cd. But we do not.

If the configuration is viewed as three-dimensional (which is the hypothesis I am suggesting) and the horizontal lines on the retina are parallel, then they should appear to be concave instead of straight. Why?

The logic of the brain is this: As a three-dimensional figure, the center triangle of the lower set is closest to the viewer. Therefore, if the horizontal lines in the external world are actually straight, then on the retina, they will be concave with the points receding on triangles that are further in the distance. Since the horizontal lines on the retina are not concave, the lines must actually not be straight which is what we experience as the illusion.

Size and distance illusions

One of the Ames demonstrations from Princeton University shows two balloons of equal size against a dark background. When one balloon expands, the other contracts, but we do not see a change in size — rather we see an illusion in which the expanding balloon seems to move towards us and the contracting balloon seems to move away from the observer. As the balloons expand and contract, they are "seen" to move back and forth from us in a rhythmic motion.

Even though the context has no information about distance, we seem to superimpose an assumption about depth anyway. The illusion would probably vanish if we witnessed two children standing side by side inflating and deflating each balloon. Then, of course, distance would be clearly defined and we would see the balloons change size.

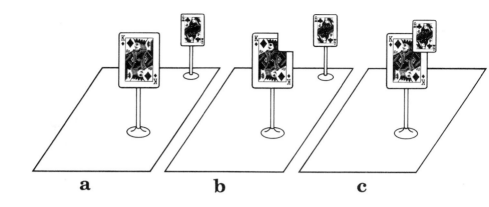

Figure 15

Figure 15. Source: Kretch and Crutchfield, page 138.

In a study reported by Kretch and Crutchfield, *size* and *distance* were placed in conflict in the following situation: Two playing cards were inserted on stands that look like the price cards on a dime store counter as shown in Figure 15. The card in the foreground had its corner cut-out so that the entire playing card on the stand in the distance fit neatly into the missing section.

The observer, however, does not see the front card as having its corner removed and another playing card behind in the distance. Rather, you see an illusion in which the distant card is seen as being smaller in size than the front card and attached to the top corner of the closer card.

The left brain's logic, I believe, works like this: On the retina, the queen appears smaller than the king which means either that there is an actual size difference between the cards or the cards are at different distances from the observer. Since the queen overlaps the king, this means that the queen cannot be farther away from the observer than the king. If the queen is not farther away, then the only remaining possibility is that the queen is actually *smaller* than the king which is what we experience (and call an illusion).

Logic similar to the playing cards was probably operating in the distorted room in which a child and an adult change physical size immediately just by walking back and forth in a room. The cue of distance was eliminated by building a trick room in which the child and the adult appear on the retina to be standing at the back wall of the room at an equal distance from the observer. When distance vanishes as an explanation, the only remaining possibility is that the child and the adult increased and decreased in physical size. (However improbable and unbelievable that is, based on our entire life experience, we instantly experience the change in size as reality.)

However, if we permit distance to be reintroduced as a possibility, the illusion will instantly disappear. For example, when the observer is allowed to poke at the walls of the trick room with a pointer while looking at the child and the adult, the illusion tends to vanish. But, if the observer is taken on a tour of the trick room to examine how the deception was accomplished, that "true knowledge" of the situation achieved in the tour will not influence the power of the illusion when the observer returns to view the scene though the peephole.

This suggests to me that the left brain's logic depends upon *immediate sensory input* from the right brain rather than memory. There is evidence for an immediate sensory input hypothesis from an interesting article published back in 1895 in a distinguished journal called the *Psychological Review*. In that article, a researcher named R. W. Wood described what he called the "Haunted Swing" illusion.

The "Haunted Swing" illusion was presented to the public at the midwinter fair in San Francisco circa 1895. Picture a spacious room with heavy Victorian furniture such as a sofa, table, chairs, a massive iron safe, and a highly-polished grand piano. Suspended from the ceiling of the room there is a huge swing which seats forty people.

The illusion is that although the swing is at rest with some forty people sitting on it, the swing seems to increase in motion moving to-and-fro, faster-and-faster, in a wider and wider arc until at one point, the participants feel the swing move up in the air and turn everyone on the swing upside down as it makes a frightening 360 degree revolution.

Wood reported that even though people knew the "secret" of the room (which was that the swing was stationary while the room, with the heavy furniture bolted to the floor, was in motion), "it was impossible to quench the sensation of 'goneness within' with each apparent rush of the swing." Then, Wood remarked in his article that when he shut his eyes, the sensation of motion *immediately disappeared.* Here, it seems to me, is an observation which has crucial implications for understanding how the left brain evaluates incoming data. The powerful illusion of motion vanished instantly when the participant closed his eyes to shut out the visual experience. Apparently, *immediate sensory input* is critical in the millisecond process of cerebral logic.

The illusion of movement

In a classic study by researcher J. F. Brown, observers squinted through a peephole to see black circles moving endlessly on a moving belt. In an adjacent peephole, you observed black circles twice the size of the ones you just viewed. The task of the observer is to adjust the speed of the larger circles until they are moving at the same velocity as the smaller circles.

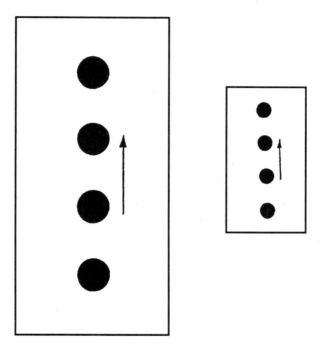

Figure 16: Source: Kretch and Crutchfield, page 125

The result was that the speed of the larger circles was reduced by the observers to one-half the speed of the smaller circles. Why?

The left brain evaluates the sensory data as follows: First, the left brain decides that the large black circles are closer to the observer than the small black circles. Therefore, if identical objects at different distances are to appear to travel at the same velocity, the ones that are closer must be reduced in speed.

Brown repeated the experiment, with this variation: The circles in both displays were of *equal size,* but one was *brighter* in intensity compared with the other. The brain translates brightness into a distance cue, especially when the context is barren. Hence, the brighter circles are interpreted as being closer to the observer, and must, therefore, be reduced in speed to match the velocity of the dimmer circles.

Brightness illusion

If you cut out two small squares from a piece of gray paper and put one square on a white background and the other on a black background, you will observe a peculiar result. The gray square on the white background will appear to be darker than the identical gray square on the black background. This illusion is so remarkable that you must experience it to believe. In the faces you will see next, you will have a chance to experience the "brightness" illusion.

In the Figure 17, the puzzle is this: All the faces you are looking at are of identical gray; yet, those faces on a lighter background appear to be darker than those faces on a darker background.

The left brain, I believe, reasons as follows: First, the brain assumes that the illumination on each face is the same as the illumination on the background. However, the illumination is least on the face in frame A; then the next in illumination is the face in frame B and so on with

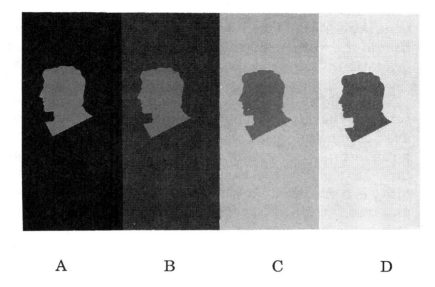

A   B   C   D

Figure 17: Source: Kretch and Crutchfield, page 79

the face in frame D having the greatest illumination.

The left brain has three possible options for evaluating the grayness of the faces. First, if the faces are of identical gray and if the illumination is least for the A face, it should appear on the retina to be darker than the B face which should appear on the retina to be darker than the C face, etc. Since, on the retina, face A is not darker than face B which is not darker than face C, etc., the brain concludes that all the faces are not of identical gray.

Next, if the illumination is least on face A and face A was actually the darkest face, with face B the next in illumination and also the next in darkness, and so on with face D having the brightest illumination and the lightest gray, then on the retina, face A should have the darkest gray followed by face B followed by face C, etc. Since the faces, on the retina, do not follow a progression of darkness from face A to Face D, the brain concludes that in the world external to the observer, there is not a gradation of gray from dark to light starting with face A.

The left brain has eliminated two possible interpretations: The left brain has concluded (a) that the faces are not of equal grayness and (b) the faces do not have a gradation of gray in which face A is the darkest and face D is the lightest. Hence, the only remaining possibility is a gradation in which face A is the lightest gray and face D is the darkest — and that is what the brain chooses to "see" which is, of course, the illusion.

Color illusions

Let's start with a striking fact about color — and that is that the experience of color is a product of the brain and does not exist in the electromagnetic continuum of light. For example, consider the "primary" colors of red, yellow, and blue. We call these "primary" because supposedly they are "pure" rather than a "mixture" of other colors.

The remarkable fact is that there are no markers — no breaks — nothing distinctive in the waves themselves* or at the " boundary" lines of the physical wave lengths of light that correspond to our "seeing" a primary color such as red and then yellow and then blue. (In fact, linguists have demonstrated that the experience of color varies from culture to culture with some tribes of people who do not see the primary colors as we

*This is analogous to the *phoneme* in linguistics. The phoneme is the smallest change in sound that signals a change in meaning. For example, compare the word "sit" with the word "hit." Curiously, there is no easily identifiable marker in the physical acoustic signal that corresponds to phonemes. In other words, the phonome has no clear-cut, physical representation in the external world of sound waves.

experience them at all.)

Another intriguing fact is that our species is capable of receiving only a pinpoint of the signals transmitted from the electromagnetic continuum. For instance, our eyes are only sensitive to 16 millionth of an inch on a continuum that is 18 1/2 miles in length. Using another measurement, if the electromagnetic continuum was a line on a fishing pole, you could unreel it 300 billion miles into space but the human species is only able to receive signals from *one mile* on the continuum.

Next, another fact: Those primary colors located opposite each other, on the color circle formed by arranging wave lengths in a perimeter from 380 to 700, will produce gray if mixed. Now, here is the illusion: Why does a *gray* patch on a *yellow* background become transformed into bluish tints?

I believe the left brain interprets the input as follows: Gray can be created by combining primary colors of light that are opposite such as yellow and blue.* In this combination the wave lengths cancel each other such as this:

Gray equals Yellow (580 mu) minus Blue (480 mu). Next, the gray patch is taken by the left brain to be part of the yellow background. If the grey is part of the yellow, then,

Yellow (580 mu) — Gray (Yellow — Blue) = Blue

or

*We have all had the experience of mixing *yellow* and *blue* paint to get green. There is no contradiction with mixing yellow and blue light to get grey. The mixing of paint produces different effects from mixing of light.

$$\text{Yellow} \quad - \quad \text{Yellow} \; + \; \text{Blue} \; = \; \text{Blue}$$

The identical logic applies to this phenomenon: A *gray* patch on a *blue* background is "seen" as having yellowish tints.

$$\text{Gray} = \text{Yellow} \; (580 \, \text{mu}) \; \text{minus} \; \text{Blue} \; (480 \, \text{mu})$$

then,

$$\text{if} \; \text{Yellow} \quad - \quad \text{Gray} \; = \; \text{Blue,}$$

then

$$\text{Yellow} \; = \; \text{Blue} \; + \; \text{Grey}$$

$$\text{Hence,} \; \text{Blue} \; + \; \text{Gray} \; (\text{Yellow} - \text{Blue}) \; = \; \text{Yellow}$$

The brain seems to be capable of lightning-calculations using algebraic relationships.

Natural life situations

The high-speed logic of the brain can be observed outside the laboratory in the behavior of children. Even casual observations show the working of the brain as, for instance, when nine-year-old David, the son of a colleague came up to his father while we were talking and asked, "Daddy, why is Jim taller than you? Is he older than you are?" From David's perspective, he observes that as children progress from grade to grade, they become older and taller. Hence, why wouldn't the correlation between age and height continue for everyone?

Spontaneous logic of the left brain can be observed in children's grammar. It is not uncommon, for example, to hear young children say, "I buyed some gum at the store" and "Who are those mans?" The use of "buyed" as the past tense of "buy" and "mans" as the plural of "man" are logically correct.

A child once asked me, if "soda" is spelled, s-o-d-a, why isn't "sewed" spelled, "s-o-d"? Of course, there is no answer. From the point of view of pure logic, the children are exactly on-target. Another child expressed this logical analysis to his mother, "I don't want to grow up. I always want to be a child because then you and Daddy will always be exactly as you are. You will never grow old and die."

SUMMARY

The illusions which first became a topic of interest to research psychologists circa 1895, give us more insight into brainswitching. I believe that the "illusion" is the end-product of the left brain's evaluation of patterns sent across the corpus callosum by the right brain. The patterns have conflicting cues which are resolved in lightning-speed with pure logic by the left brain.

The patterns register on the retina of the eye and a logical computation is instantly performed with some built-in programmed assumptions, such as the premise that many two-dimensional patterns imply depth as, for instance, the upper half of a vertical line is farther away from the observer while the lower half of the line is closer to the observer.

The logic of the left brain is visible in the utterances of children which adults often find amusing. What amuses us is that we recognize that a child's conclusion may be false, but the process of deriving the conclusion was logical.

REFERENCES

Allport, F. H. *Theories of Perception and the Concept of Structure.* New York: Wiley, 1955.

Ames, A. Binocular vision as affected by relations between uniocular stimulus-patterns in commonplace environments. *American Journal of Psychology,* 1946, *59,* 333-357.

Ames, A. Visual perception and the rotating trapezoidal window. *Psychological Monograph,* 1951, # 324.

Boring, E. G. Sensation and Perception in the *History of Experimental Psychology.* Appleton-Century-Crofts, New York, 1942.

Brown, J. F. The visual perception of velocity. *Psychol. Forsch.,* 1931, 14, 199-232.

Ittelson, W. H. Size as a cue to distance; static localization. *American Journal of Psychology,* 1951, *64,* 54-67.

Ittelson, W. H. *The Ames Demonstrations in Perception.* Princeton University Press, Princeton, 1952.

Kretch, D., and Crutchfield, R. S. *Elements of Psychology.* New York: Knopf, 1955.

Müller-Lyer, F. C. Ueber Kontrast und Konfluxion. Z. Psychol., 1896, *9,* 1-16.

CHAPTER 4

WORK AND PLAY

ONE OF THE GREAT MYSTERIES OF HUMAN BEHAVIOR

The twenty four hour day can be divided into three parts: work, play, and sleep. We seem to dedicate about eight hours for work, eight hours for play and about eight hours for sleep. On the surface, the boundary lines between these three activities seem to be transparent. "Work" hours are those measured in monetary compensation when we are "on duty", while hours that we "spend" in "play" means that we are "off" meaning "off duty." During play time we are free to do as we please with no rules, no restrictions, no confinement, and no structure to our activity.

The purest meaning of play is to observe the activity of pre-school children. They are free to pursue an activity with or without rules, with or without a goal, with or without a connection to reality. They can start and stop an activity at will. They can shift from one activity to another without a penalty. At the climax of the "play" activity, there is no "pay-off" as in a paycheck.

For the purest meaning of work, we must observe adults. Adults seem to have sharp lines of demarcation for the beginning and ending of the activity called "work." Often the starting and ending hours are documented with the stamping of a time clock. These hours are associated with money as in the expression, "time is money." One can visualize a meter running as in a taxi cab. Often people say, "my time is worth — dollars" meaning each "work" hour can be traded for X number of dollars.

About work,* people often say," I must be at work today at 8 A.M." *"I must..."* is a frequent expression when people refer to work activity. This implies that there is a *discipline* associated with the hours one works. And discipline implies *duty, focus of attention, paying attention, seriousness,* and a *penalty for error.* There is continued attention beyond the limit of interest.

There is continued attention even when one feels the need to "escape" the activity which comes when one experiences noxious signals such as boredom, fatigue, and tedium. Those *noxious signals,* incidentally, may be an attempt by our physiological system to prevent damage by motivating us to discontinue an activity that is moving us into a harmful region.

Nevertheless, we usually ignore the noxious signals and continue the "work" activity until we reach a predesignated stopping point. In fact, discipline means that we have trained ourselves to either tune-out noxious signals or diminish the volume of the signals to the faintest possible level of transmission. Not only have we trained ourselves, as adults, to ignore noxious signals, we have, starting in adolescence, expanded boundary lines which, when reached, trigger noxious signals.

For example, we say that children have a "short attention span." Notice that children begin an activity, the noxious signals go off, and they escape by rapidly shifting to another activity. Gradually, as children

*My colleague, Dr. Milton Andersen, feels that what I call "work" is better described as a "job." Work to him is simply changing something into something else. Work is a transformation process that is pleasurable, but a job has the confinement and other features presented in this chapter.

"mature" they become more skillful in delaying those signals. The school experience seems to be especially valuable in helping children develop skill in enlarging the space within the boundaries of an activity — almost like a balloon that expands and expands before the noxious signals flash on.

However, *all activities are neutral.* What makes an activity perceived as "work" or "play" is a function of how each side of the brain processes information. Further, if we understand how the brain concludes that an activity is work or play, we can, I believe, alter conditions, at will, to create an experience that is either work or play. The implications for human behavior are enormous because nested within the conditions that create a perception of either work or play is the *secret of motivation.*

My hypothesis is that the perception of work is a by-product of the left brain and the perception of play is a by-product of the right brain.

Work, work, work — what is work?

Is there a physical reality to work? Both executives and laborers can feel exhausted from a day's work. Yet when we apply physiological measures to assess how much work has been done, *only the person doing physical tasks* shows a dramatic change in all indicators including breathing, pulse rate, blood pressure, temperature, oxygen consumption, muscle contraction, and chemical changes in the blood. On all the measures, there is almost an undetectable reading for executives.

If work does not have a physical reality, then let's explore how people perceive work compared with play.

I asked college students in several classes to list the differences and similarities between work and play. Here are the results:

The students associated these characteristics with work

It is done for pay.

It is done to satisfy basic needs.

It is punitive.

It is regular.

It is done within time limits that are usually set by others.

It is compulsory.

It has boundaries.

It is involuntary.

It is supervised.

It is drudgery.

It is associated with worry and pressure.

It is hard.

It requires individual discipline.

It is done away from home.

It involves competition.

It is a means to an end.

It is supervised by others.

It produces a product which one may not care about.

It is something you don't want to do.

It is required.

It may be repetitious.

Others view it as "good".

It is expected by society.

It involves many responsibilities.

It is structured.

It is necessary.

One may want to discontinue it.

It is productive.

It is tense.

It is serious.

The difficulty with the associations that people have with the concept of work is that it is rather easy to find examples of play which have characteristics in the list.

For example, in play, there can be boundaries, pressure, difficulty, competition, supervision (i.e. referee), rules, time limits, anxiety, fear-of-failure, pride, compulsion, structure, tension, seriousness, a restrictive environment and so forth. But, if it is play, then the task is not punitive; it is not unenjoyable; it does not have "genuine" stress; it is not unsatisfying; and it is not drudgery. If it is play, the activity has *positive affect*.

The only feature that differentiates play from work is that *one feels good about it* — the feeling tone is definitely positive. One is elated rather than depressed. One feels rejuvenated rather than depleted. One feels energy rather than fatigue. One seeks the activity rather than flees from it. One is attracted to the task rather than repelled by it. There is approach rather than avoidance.

Let's test this hypothesis by examining the characteristics that the students associated with play.

You pay rather than being paid.

It is unsupervised.

It is unstructured.

It is non-productive.

It is relaxing.

You control it.

It is satisfying.

It is voluntary.

It is enjoyable.

It is self-compensating.

The means is the end.

The process rather than end-product is the goal.

It has intrinsic pleasure.

It can be discontinued at any time.

It is non-repetitive.

It is unscheduled.

It gives immediate satisfaction.

It is an escape mechanism.

It has no boundaries.

It is non-serious.

It is easy.

It does not require self-discipline.

It can be done anywhere.

It has variety.

It can be nonsensical.

Brainswitching to produce work or play

One-third of our time is for sleep; one-third is for play and one-third is for work. Two-thirds of our time involves either work or play, yet we have no clear-cut concept of what conditions produce these two seemingly mutually exclusive activities — if, indeed, they are mutually exclusive.

When is work work and when is play play? The boundaries are fuzzy. It would seem that any activity could be either work or play, depending upon whether participants view themselves as a worker or a player.

It is interesting that the business community vaguely recognizes that any activity may be transformed from work into play, but the precise alchemy to perform this magic is not yet known. Yet, business has attempted in rather primitive ways to transform work into play with strategies such as music-while-you-work, coffee breaks, job enrichment (for variety), job rotation (to relieve boredom), pay incentives, job sharing, and flextime. These are attempts to "enhance job satisfaction" which it is thought will increase "efficiency and productivity." The data show, incidentally, that there is only a low correlation between job satisfaction and productivity.

Apparently, workers can experience great job satisfaction and yet productivity is low. Conversely, employees can feel little job satisfaction and be highly productive. Intuitively, one would expect that job satisfaction and productivity should be highly correlated, but they are not. These two variables seem to be almost independent.

Perhaps the definition of work that most people would agree upon is that work is any activity for which one receives money. If we perform a task for money, then it is work. The problem is that often, activity for which we are paid is perceived as play and leisure activities which most would identify as play is perceived by many people as work.

As a personal example, my father, who was a successful manager of his own business seemed to perceive his work as play and leisure activities such as playing cards or other games as hard work. A shipyard superintendent that I once interviewed, told me that his work is definitely his play. He preferred working to any other activity. He looked forward to work everyday and "hated" that time when he had to take a vacation. A vacation for him was "heavy duty" work.

Transforming Work into Play

The first assumption in my model of work and play is that work and play are usually perceived as mutually exclusive — they are at opposite ends of the continuum. An activity — *any activity is neutral* but will move from one end of the continuum to the other depending upon certain variables which we will explore next.

The gain-loss (G/L) ratio. This concept states that as the ratio of gain-to-loss approaches a coefficient that is less than or equal to 1, the activity will be perceived as work. As the G/L ratio approaches a coefficient greater that 1, the activity will be perceived as play.

As an illustration, let's consider the behavior of "playing" slot machines. If gain in this situation is defined as *expected gain* (i.e., the money one may possibly win) and loss as *actual loss* (i.e., the money one inserts in the machine and the physical effort of pulling the handle), then the larger the *expected gain* in relation to the *actual loss,* the more the activity will be perceived as play. Conversely, the more the *expected gain* approaches a point where it is exactly the same or less than *actual loss,* the prediction is that the activity will be perceived as work.

It would be easy to set up an experiment to test the gain-to-loss hypothesis, but the results seem transparent. For example, from the model my prediction is that people will continue to "play" the slot machine significantly longer when the gain-to-loss ratio is that the " player" has a chance of winning $5 every time one cent is inserted in the slot and the handle pulled compared with another machine in which the "player" has a chance of winning five cents every time one cent is inserted and the handle is pulled. In fact, my prediction is that the frequency of "playing" a machine will decrease systematically as the G/L ratio moves from a coefficient substantially greater than 1 to a coefficient that approaches or is equal to 1.

As a practical example, thirty years ago, programmed learning was ushered in as a panacea that would solve all educational problems by accelerating learning, producing long-term retention, and drilling students on fundamentals thereby freeing instructors to help students achieve higher level concepts. Further, since students worked at their own pace until mastery was accomplished, each student earned an "A."

Interestingly, programmed learning was actually effective in accelerating learning, producing long-term retention, drilling students on fundamentals, and allowing students to progress at their own pace until mastery was obtained. Most studies showed that programmed learning produced significantly better results compared with traditional approaches such as lectures or textbooks. However, like the dinosaurs, programmed learning is now almost extinct. Why?

The reason can be explained with the gain-to-loss ratio. In programmed learning, information was presented to the student in small amounts called frames each of which contained a sentence or two of information. After the student viewed a frame, a response was required such as answering a question.

Most formal studies designed to evaluate programmed learning showed that for almost all topics from learning spelling to calculus, from learning automotive mechanics to fingering the clarinet, programmed learning was more advantageous than a teacher explaining a concept or a student reading textbooks or a student writing answers in a workbook. But, although programmed learning was a productive experience, students complained that "working" through a program frame-by-frame by reading each frame and then writing a response to demonstrate competency was tedious and boring.

The activity was not attractive. In fact, it was so noxious that students wanted to escape. The frame-by-frame reading and writing was perceived as extremely hard work. Hence, programmed learning disappeared from the educational scene.

Student perception of programmed learning as "heavy duty labor" is predictable from a gain-to-loss ratio because the information transmitted by a frame was usually equal to or even less than the input by the student. It was analogous to asking students to "play" a slot machine in which they insert one cent with the expectation of winning two cents. This moved the activity to an extreme point at the the work end of the play-work continuum.

Programmed learning could have survived by changing the G/L ratio to move the activity in the direction of play. This is accomplished by increasing the gain in relation to the "loss" (that is, the input by the student). For example, the power of programmed learning was that the person creating the program was supposed to test a version of the program with a group of students, analyze their written responses to each frame, then rewrite every frame in which more than 5% of the students made errors. The program creator would then test the rewritten version with another group of students and so forth until 95% of the students responded perfectly to every single frame in the program.

This strategy for developing a program was more rigorous than the development, for instance, of any textbook. The procedure for developing a program insured that the presentation of information was optimal for communicating with the students. Most textbooks, by comparison, are rarely tested to discover whether students understand all sections in the book. That's why instructors are needed — to explain passages that are confusing or incomprehensible to students.

Since a program went through so many revisions until the coefficient of communication was maximum, it was not necessary for the final version to be presented to the student frame-by-frame in small bits of information that required a written response by the student after each and every frame. The final version could have been presented as a book that the student reads chapter-by-chapter with perhaps self-test questions at the end of each chapter.

The end-product should have been a traditional book because the content could be understood instantly in one reading by most students — a feature never attained in any conventional textbook. Notice that the activity would then have moved from work to play since there would be a gigantic gain when students internalize huge chunks of understanding in a single reading.

Genuiness of loss. The denominator of the gain-to-loss ratio is, of course, loss. But, "loss" is not obvious. The loss associated with work is different from the loss associated with play. The "loss" perceived in the context of work can be characterized as an "actual" loss. It is a genuine loss. It is real. Not only is it real, but it will vary from individual to individual. For example, to the multi-millionaire, J.P. Morgan, a loss may not be perceived as genuine or real until it was of the magnitude of fifty million dollars; but to a college student, a loss may be real, perceptually, when it is fifty dollars.

At the play end of the continuum, there is no genuine loss; there is no actual loss; there is no real loss. Perhaps the most accurate way of expressing this concept is to say that in the context of play, "loss" is perceived as *genuine and non-genuine simultaneously.* It is a **real** and a **fantasy** loss simultaneously. For example, if a player in a game should become upset at "losing," another player is apt to comment, "Relax, remember it's only a game." It's only a game meaning that you lost but you didn't really lose. This paradox of enjoying reality and fantasy simultaneously seems to be unique to play. In play, "you have your cake and eat it, too."

If the left brain concludes that a loss is genuine, then the activity will be perceived as work. For instance, "players" of professional sports are aware that every mistake made is a loss of income and perhaps the loss of one's livelihood, and hence the activity is perceived as work — hard work.* If the left brain concludes that the loss is non-genuine, then there is no loss; there is no penalty, and the activity then moves into the play zone of the right brain.

*In a recent television interview, the coach of a professional team commented, "Players are not paid to play the game; they are paid to win."

The right brain *can function* with *mutually exclusive* events. It can operate with contradictions because the right brain is non-evaluative. It is non-judgmental. Hence, on the right side of the brain, one can experience loss and non-loss simultaneously, as is characteristic of games.

The risk paradox. At the extreme end of the work continuum, risk is maximum; but at the play end, there is a paradox in which risk and non-risk occur simultaneously. The risk paradox can be observed in people playing games (except professional athletes) because players have the expectation that, "If I win the game, there is a handsome gain; but if I lose, there is no real loss."

Years ago, I worked with a team of psychologists who attempted to cope with the risk paradox to solve this problem: Air Force flight crews who made forced landings in the frozen wilderness of the Arctic often exhibited puzzling behavior. In this traumatic situation, crews highly skilled in survival training acted as if all prior training was completely erased from their awareness.

For example, in survival training, flight crews practice over and over in the creative use of the plane and every item in it. Fuel, for instance can be used for a fire and parachutes can be used as insulators to keep warm. And, of course, the highest priority is to stay with the aircraft because it is easier for rescuers who are searching from the air to locate the plane.

Many crews, however, seemed to behave as if they had received *no survival training at all*. They would, for instance, try to walk away only to wander in endless circles until they were exhausted and finally died. The aircraft was often found abandoned and completely intact — no attempt had been made to use the plane or its contents as resources to survive.

The challenge for psychologists was to simulate in the laboratory the kind of crisis which would trigger the "training amnesia" which seemed to occur in Arctic crash landings. If it was possible to recreate the acute anxiety that crews experience, then perhaps training strategies could be devised to help flyers continue to function in adaptive ways no matter how severe the crisis.

The phenomenon has not yet been reproduced in the laboratory because of the risk paradox. When people are aware that they are part of a study, it is extremely difficult to produce the high-voltage anxiety that is characteristic of Arctic crash landings. The reason is that participants, in some corner of their minds, feel that "this is a play situation" no matter how traumatic it may seem. Hence, they feel unsafe and yet safe simultaneously which means that their behavior is atypical of flight crews who perceive a crisis situation as genuinely life-threatening.

When an activity is viewed by participants as a risk and a non-risk simultaneously, the activity moves into the play zone of the right brain. There is a brainswitch from the left to the right brain.

Closure. In an activity classified as play, there seems to be a definite climax — there is closure; but for an activity perceived as work, the activity may or may not have closure. For play, there is a high certainty of beginning and ending boundary lines; but in work, an activity may continue and continue day-after-day with no ending marker.

The probability of eventual drive reduction. In a game, no matter how much the tension increases, one has almost maximum certainty that eventually, usually in a short time, there will be tension reduction. The tension reduction will come in either a handsome gain or in a non-genuine loss, so that no matter what the outcome of the game, everyone "wins." With slot machines, the tension reduction occurs in seconds, and in card games the time may be several hours.

For play activity, the coefficient for eventual drive reduction approaches one (that is, there is certainty of eventual drive reduction), but for an activity perceived as work, the coefficient approaches zero. As one moves further into the zone of work, there is maximum uncertainty that tension will be reduced. For example, problems in the work zone may continue to be unsolved and unresolved day-after-day, month-after-month — even year-after-year.

People will tend to have an *extremely high tolerance* for tension while they are in the zone of play activity because they are certain that eventually the tension will be reduced when the answer is given, the game is over, or the riddle is revealed. In the work zone, however, tolerance for tension may be significantly lower because one is uncertain when, if ever, the tension will be reduced.

Drive magnification. Since one is certain that eventually, tension will be reduced in a play activity, one may *seek ways to magnify the tension.* If the activity is play, then one will be attracted to drive induction and drive magnification. There is pleasure in tension induction and in tension magnification because one is assured that eventually, when the boundary of the activity is reached — usually in a short time, there will be climax to the tension. It will disappear. It will reduce to zero. The classic example is sexual activity.

When one experiences great uncertainty about the eventual reduction of tension, one tends to escape the activity. This may be a factor which differentiates individuals who are highly creative from less creative people. The creative person searches for conundrums (Asher, 1963) and then magnifies the tension by continuing to toy with what seems to be an insolvable problem. The creative person probably feels intuitively, perhaps as a result of past problem solving success, that eventually a solution will be discovered, revealed or invented. The creative person expects with high certainty that tension reduction will occur when the problem is resolved. Therefore, the activity is perceived as play. The behavior of any inventor such as Thomas Edison illustrates this phenomenon.

When Edison was searching for the secret of the electric light, he tried thousands of possibilities for a workable filament including a strand of his own hair. Others had tried but given up the search with the conclusion that an electric light was impossible. No one had ever done it. It probably could not be done.

Edison continued to explore the problem in spite of failure after failure because he was certain (based on a past history of solving unsolvable problems) that it could be done. Hence, the activity was perceived as a toy — a plaything. "Failure" was not perceived as failure by Edison, but as another option that can be eliminated —

one less possibility to look at.

Certainty of gain. Curiously, the greater the expectation that one will win on every trial of an activity, the more the activity will be perceived as work. If the expectation of gain is either absolutely certain or absolutely uncertain, the activity will be perceived as work. For the expectation of gain, the middle range of curve is associated with play activities.

For example, if every time one inserts one cent in a slot machine and pulls the handle, the machine pays off with ten cents, the individual may continue the activity for a long period of time, but the "player's" perception of the activity will shift from play to work. And, the longer one "plays" the machine, the more the activity will be perceived as work that is tedious, difficult, boring, tiring, and monotonous.

As another illustration, one company discovered that "certainty of gain" may not produce the desired change in behavior. The intent was to reduce absenteeism among workers. Rewarding people every day they were on-time for work was not as effective as this procedure: Every day during the week that a person was on-time for work, the individual drew one card from a deck of shuffled cards. At the end of the week, the employee with the best poker hand, won a jackpot.

Professor B. F. Skinner, a Harvard psychologist, discovered that animals will quickly stop working at a task when regular rewards of food were discontinued. If, however, animals were not rewarded after every successful response, (but rather the rewards came sporadically on some successful responses but not others), when the rewards were discontinued, the animals continued to perform for *thousands of trials* before "giving-up."

The reality paradox. In play, there is the risk paradox in which there is a win-win situation. That is, a player either wins the game or experiences a non-genuine loss (after all, it is only a game). The reality paradox is also autistic right-brain thinking in which we can "have our cake and eat it, too."

The classic illustration of the reality paradox is the animated cartoons pioneered by the Walt Disney Movie Studio. In movie cartoons such as Popeye, Tom and Jerry, and Mr. Magoo, the sympathetic character can express aggression by inflicting physical injury on the villain and yet, the hero need not feel guilty because even though the "bad guy" experienced excruciating pain, the individual was not actually in pain.

The reality paradox can be seen in almost every scene of these "children's cartoons." For example, even a cursory inspection will show sadism within the boundaries of savagery in which the victim is mutilated as when the mouse presses the cat's head into a sizzling waffle iron which, of course, produces an agonizing scream from the cat whose cranium is irreversibly disfigured. Yet, in the next scene, the cat's head is a normal shape and there are no apparent manifestations of brain damage nor is there a trace of pain. The cat was hurt and yet not hurt simultaneously. Other macabre examples of the reality paradox would be when the "heavy" character is dismembered and yet not dismembered. decapitated and yet not decapitated, or even killed and yet, in the next scene, we see that the individual is very much alive.

Fantasy. We tend to think of fantasy as the opposite

of reality. Fantasy is unreal and reality is real. Fantasy is an imagination of "what could be" and reality is a perception of "what is." Fantasy is fiction and reality is truth. Fantasy is as fragile as the membrane of a soap bubble but reality is as solid as a rock.

Actually, I believe that reality is a special case of fantasy. Throughout human history, people have one fantasy after another which they and their contemporaries have agreed to call "reality." The clearest illustrations come from the field of medicine. The concept of germs — microbes that cause disease and kill people was viewed by physicians as a fantasy without a trace of reality. Physicians were outraged, as a matter of fact, when Sir Joseph Lister suggested that a dramatic reduction in the incidence of childbirth deaths could be achieved if attending physicians would wash their hands before touching a patient. The accepted procedure was to move from patient to patient without washing one's hands since the concept of antiseptic treatment was a "science-fiction" fantasy.

Before Lister's time, the most trivial operation was followed by infection and death in 50% of the cases. His application of antiseptics was spectacular because mortalities for all surgical procedures were reduced to less than 3%. When Lister's fantasy was perceived as "reality," it became safe for surgeons to open abdomens, chests, heads, and joints.

William Jenner, a British physician, was almost driven from the medical profession by ridicule from his contemporaries with the "theory" (translate theory as fantasy) that the lethal curse of smallpox could be eliminated by making a cut into a healthy person's skin and then smearing pus into the wound from someone infected with cowpox. This was viewed as a dangerous theory (a fantasy) created by someone who was obviously naive or perhaps even deranged. Dr. Jenner lived long enough to witness the acceptance into medical practice of the concept of inoculation which in one generation made the transition from "fantasy" to "reality."

One generation's fantasy is another generation's reality. Jules Verne created "impossible" fantasies of vehicles that fly in the air and move under water — yet later, in less that two generations, the airplane and the submarine were reality. Also, one generation's reality often become the next generation's fantasy.

For example, in 1875, the highly-respected *Scientific American* magazine published predictions made by the most eminent scientists of the day. These scientists forecasted that a serious, overwhelming problem for human beings in the year 1900 — which was only 25 years away was this: The number of horses in New York City would increase geometrically with the population so that by 1900, the city would be in danger of sinking into the ocean under the weight of horse manure. The scientists did not foresee that an alternative to horse-drawn transportation would appear.

What is "scientific" reality for one generation may be fiction for the next generation. When the steam locomotive was first proposed, leading scientists of the day warned that the train would never be practical because it was a scientific fact that human beings could not breathe at speeds of 30 miles per hour.

Today, it is a "scientific fact" that "the human organism can only cut two sets of teeth, the "baby" teeth and

the "adult" teeth. This concept is perceived as reality —
but is it?

The "fact" about human teeth seems to be valid only
because we have observed no contradictory cases. But,
in the August 8, 1965 issue of the *San Francisco
Chronicle,* there was a small news item captioned,
"Woman, 65, is teething."

Mrs. Fanny Williams from Stonewall, Mississippi
had trouble, the Chronicle reported, with her false
teeth, so she went to a dentist. The dentist discovered
that the 65 year old woman was growing another set of
teeth. So far, four upper and one lower teeth have
emerged.

Play and work, I am suggesting, is not a contrast
between fantasy and reality but rather a contrast
between *divergent* and *convergent* fantasy. Play has
divergent fantasy because there are usually many,
many options or many strategies that are possible in the
play activity; but in work, the activity tends to be
perceived as a monolithic fantasy with only one way "to
play the game." Of course, divergent thinking is characteristic of the right brain and convergent thinking
seems to be the style of the left brain.

Clinical psychologists picture schizophrenia as an
escape into fantasy in which one prefers a dream world
to reality. If the schizophrenia escapes into fantasy,
then the workaholic can be conceptualized as an *escape
into reality*. The only fantasy that is attractive to the
workaholic is the fantasy of work.

How work and play are related to brainswitching

The activity we perceive as *work* is a convergent "fantasy" in which one step follows another in a logical and predictable pattern. Predictability is important because work activity must coordinate with others who are involved in work activities. The logical, methodical, one-step-at-a-time pattern suggests that an activity perceived as work is comfortable being played out in the left brain.

As further evidence that work is a left brain activity, Stanford professor, Tom Peters observes that the smallest, most trivial change in a work procedure tends to be upsetting to workers from the mail clerk to the president of the company. This is understandable since the left brain is spooked by novelty, no matter how trivial the change may be. The left brain wants a stable, consistent, predictable pattern.

The activity we perceive as play is a divergent fantasy in which contradictions are not only permitted but welcomed. Play is a kind of Alice in Wonderland of contradictions which are not perceived as contradictions at all but rather normal parameters of the activity. For instance, in play there is the presence of a genuine and non-genuine loss simultaneously. We often feel safe and unsafe simultaneously as I illustrated in the risk paradox.

In play, we experience reality and fantasy simultaneously as shown in the reality paradox. Being comfortable with contradictions seems to be characteristic of the right brain as evidenced in night dreams in which contradictions are accepted as logical and realistic.

The brainswitching seems to be this: When an activity moves into the left brain, it tends to be perceived as work and when it shifts into the right brain, it is perceived as play. I will further illustrate the brainswitching that creates a perception of work or play in the chapters on learning languages and learning mathematics. As we understand more and more how the variables I have described operate together, we will have increased skill in brainswitching the perception of an activity from work to play.

REFERENCES

Asher, J. J. Toward a neo-field theory of problem solving. *Journal of General Psychology,* 1963, *68*, 3-8.

Asher, J.J. Toward a neo-field theory of behavior. *Journal of Humanistic Psychology,* 1964, *4*(2), 85-94.

Peters, T. New workplace turns change into a ho-hum affair. *San Jose Mercury News,* p 4f, January 28, 1988.

CHAPTER 5

BRAINSWITCHING

AN APPLICATION TO COUNSELING

Most conventional psychotherapies are based on **talk** and therefore play to the left brain. Typically, the counselor sits down with the client and *discusses* the problem. A counseling relationship can take many forms as, for instance, the counselor will *listen* carefully to what the individual is saying, then mirror the thoughts and feelings of the person. The counselor becomes a *mirror* by verbally reflecting back to the client the nuances of the individual's thoughts. For instance, the counselor may say, "In other words, you feel that your mother manipulated you be feigning illness."

The counselor becomes a "sounding board" that echoes the individual's thoughts and feelings. In playing back the client's thinking and feelings, the individual has a chance to explore and reevaluate in order to achieve a fresh view of troubling relationships. The value of skillful listening is that individuals are able, in theory, eventually to solve their own problems. This is called **non-directive therapy.**

Another variation of the left brain counseling approach is for the counselor to *listen* to the individual explain a problem, then to *suggest* solutions. This approach is called ***directive therapy.*** Dr. Joseph Wolpe, who is Professor of Psychiatry at the Temple University School of Medicine, has concluded[1] that any conventional "talking" therapy either non-directive or directive results in improvement in about 50% of the cases. The chances of an individual improving in a left-brain oriented "talking" approach is a flip of the coin—that is, one chance in two.

According to Dr. Wolpe and others,[2] the odds for improvement can be increased from one chance in two which is the flip of the coin to 8 chances in 10 if the counseling technique shifts from talking to action. Dr. Wolpe call his action-oriented therapy, "behavior therapy."[3]

Brainswitching from the left brain to the right in behavior therapy has been effective for a wide-range of disturbing behavior such as *phobias* (an exaggerated fear of harmless persons, places and things), *ritualized behavior* as, for instance, washing one's hands every few minutes and other disturbances including *asthma, depression, anxiety, migraine headaches, stammering, frigidity and impotency.*

To illustrate how brainswitching works, some case histories will be presented.

Phobia

A phobia that is quite common is an exaggerated fear of spiders. Researcher Isaac M. Marks reported a brainswitching technique called "flooding,"[4] which was used successfully to "erase" the fear of spiders in the case of M.A. It works like this:

M.A. sat in a comfortable chair and was asked to **imagine**[5] as vividly as possible that she was alone in a room while black hairy spiders bite her as they crawl up her legs and arms and then entered her mouth and nose. During this frightening scene which lasted an hour, M.A. was to see herself screaming uncontrollably and helplessly. The intent is to produce **maximum** anxiety for as long as possible. When the individual is placed in prolonged and inescapable contact with the frightening entity, anxiety should reach a peak and exhaust itself. This is the technique of *flooding*.

The degree of anxiety during the ordeal is monitored by observations of outward behaviors such as grimaces and clenching of fists, by the person's own account of individual's experience, and by physical instrumentation that records skin resistance and heart rate.

As soon as the anxiety seems to be disappearing, the therapist introduces new variations in the frightening spider scenario. For homework, M.A. was asked to relive many times the "scary" fantasy that created uncontrollable anxiety.

After a few sessions, the panic reaction to the horrible fantasies of spiders will vanish. And the person is now ready to confront a real life situation. For example, the therapist held a spider in his hand and asked M.A. to touch "this dangerous creature that will bite her slowly and painfully." [6]

After about ten sessions of flooding in fantasy and four experiences of actual physical contact with spiders, three of four individuals improved and their non-fear of spiders continued when the people were followed-up one year later.

Another variation of brainswitching is *desensitization* as illustrated by the case of B.L.[7] who had an unmanageable fear of cats. She received two sessions of flooding in fantasy. Each session was two hours in length after which she expressed a readiness to experience real cats. At this time, a black cat was placed on a table about six feet away from her. As B.L. looked at the cat, she felt intense tachycardia (rapid heart action and acute anxiety) that lasted for five minutes.

Over the next five minutes, the therapist encouraged B.L. in a *reassuring manner* to continue looking at the cat while gradually, the cat was moved closer to her. Every movement of the cat in B.L.'s direction triggered a momentary increase in tachycardia and the sensation of anxiety. But, after fifteen minutes, she was able to touch the cat and eventually, she was able to stroke the cat and hold it on her lap. Finally, at the end of a two hour session, B.L. was cuddling the cat on her lap without experiencing anxiety.

In *desensitization*, the therapist helps the person to experience muscular relaxation as the feared entity is gradually moved closer and closer. When the desensitization approach was used in a pilot study with ten people[8] who had severe, specific phobias such as an extreme fear of dogs, cats, spiders, or balloons, all of the individuals experienced a significant reduction in their fear after brainswitching. Before treatment, the average score for the fear was **7.3** which decreased to **5.7** after the flooding in fantasy; and then the fear was further reduced to **2.4** after desensitization.[9]

Treatment in actual exposure to the feared entity, at first from a distance and then gradually moving closer and closer had more influence in fear reduction than treatment in fantasy. No relapses were reported when the people were contacted in later follow-up interviews.

Ritualisitc Behavior

Some people feel that unless they perform a certain ritual "something terrible will happen." For example, one may fear contamination from touching anything and therefore the person must wash his hands every few minutes during the day. Janet[10] recorded fourteen "accidental cures" of people with ritualistic compulsions while the people were in the Military Service. Apparently, if one is in an inescapable situation in which the person is blocked from performing the ritual, the compulsion may disappear.

Researchers, S.R. Rachman[11] and his colleagues randomly assigned ten hospitalized patients with a compulsive disorder to (a) a relaxation treatment, (b) flooding or (c) desensitization.

In flooding, for instance, a patient[12] who feared contamination from animals such as rodents was encouraged to touch them and let them run on the bed, towels, clothing and other personal belongings. The animal was even placed, for a few minutes, on the person's hair. Again, the intent of flooding is to *empty the fear* by escalating it into a peak experience that exhausts its energy.

In desensitization, the *least* feared object is presented first, and gradually objects that triggered more intense fear are introduced. For example, one patient[13] feared contamination from hospitals. The therapist selected an object such as a bandage that elicited only mild fear. The therapist would touch a bandage to his own clothes, hair, and face and then ask the patient to imitate his actions. Gradually, other objects associated with hospitals were introduced, and each aroused a higher level of fear until, after three weeks, the therapist walked up to the hospital entrance and touched an ambulance. Immediately, the patient copied the therapist's actions.

The results demonstrated that the brainswitching techniques of flooding and desensitization in real life situations produced significantly more improvement than a relaxation treatment alone. Flooding and desensitization were equally effective and in a follow-up study nine months later, the improvements continued.

"Normal" Fears

Fear may be a by-product of the left brain's attempt to keep us safe. Certainly, fear has survival value. It produces an avoidance reaction to potentially harmful stimuli in the environment.

The problem is that fear is often non-adaptive because it is triggered when the left brain makes a false evaluation that a situation is dangerous. An example is public speaking. Perhaps 60% or more of the population have a fear of speaking in front of a group of people. This fear can be so extreme that it approaches, for many people, the sensation of terror.

Professor Gordon L. Paul[14] from the University of Illinois explored ways of reducing in university students the "normal" fear of public speaking. University students were randomly divided into three groups. In one group, the counselor played to the **left brain** by *explaining* and *discussing* the fear of public speaking in an attempt to help the students view the situation as harmless. This is called an *insight-oriented* procedure.

In another group, the counselor played to the **right brain** with a desensitization technique in which the students imagined in specific detail the most threatening public speaking situation that was possible. In addition to left brain and right brain treatment groups, there were several control groups who either received a placebo of attention from a counselor or simply were on a waiting list and received no treatment at all.

The **results** showed that the students receiving a right brain treatment were the only ones having a significant reduction on measures of anxiety and the gains continued after six weeks. Even after two years, 85% of students treated with a right brain approach, showed a significant improvement compared with 50% of those with a placebo, and 22% for students who received no treatment at all.[15]

For other "normal" fears such as the panic reaction that many people feel when they must perform on a test, studies seem to confirm that a right brain approach as flooding or desensitization produces a greater reduction in fear that is longer-lasting compared with approaches that are based on talking-out the problem.

Professor Paul from the University of Illinois reviewed research studies of 90 different therapists who worked with nearly 1,000 different clients. "The findings," according to Dr. Paul, "were overwhelmingly positive, and for the first time in the history of psychological treatments, a specific therapeutic package reliably produced measurable benefits for clients across a broad range of distressing problems in which anxiety was of fundamental importance." He added, " . . . 'relapse' and 'symptom substitution' were notably lacking . . ."[16]

Why brainswitching works

At the beginning of this chapter, I described conventional psychotherapies that, in my opinion, play to the left brain in an attempt to erase distressing behavior such as fear and anxiety. In one conventional approach, the counselor is *silent* most of the time, listens skillfully to what the client is saying, then *reflects* back the client's thoughts and feelings. This is called *non-directive therapy*. Another conventional approach is *directive therapy* in which the counselor discusses the problem with the client and offers specific suggestions in an attempt to resolve the difficulty.

A right brain technique, I am suggesting, is *behavior therapy* that attempts to work *directly* with changing the client's behavior on the promise that when behavior is altered, thoughts and feelings will follow with a dramatic change. This is consistent with the concept that the left brain is monitoring the individual's physical behavior and then making an evaluation.

"Facts" are created through experiences which the left brain cannot deny. It is easy for the left brain to refute assertions and suggestions by counselors, but difficult to invalidate factual information coming from physical experiences. This is consistent, incidentally, with the famous James-Lange Theory of Emotion which states that we do not run because we are afraid, *we are afraid because we run.* The automatic physical response comes **before** the emotional feeling.

Professor Adolph O. DiLoreto of Western Michigan University conducted a thorough and carefully designed study[17] to compare the effectiveness of three therapeutic procedures.

One hundred college undergraduates from Michigan State University volunteered to participate in this project because they were experiencing acute anxiety which they wanted to eliminate. Each student was given an extensive battery of tests before, during, and after treatment in one of the three therapeutic procedures. The students were again evaluated three months after the treatment.

The **results** showed that a brainswitching behavior therapy was significantly more effective in reducing anxiety than either of the left brain approaches. For instance, there was approximately 30% more anxiety reduction with a right brain therapeutic strategy. Furthermore, the gains held when students were checked three months later.

The left brain therapies were about equal in reducing anxiety which was significantly lower compared with students who were untreated.

Paradoxical Therapy: Another effective brainswitching technique

About 50 years ago, the Viennese psychiatrist, Dr. Viktor Frankl turned conventional "talking" therapies inside-out by suggesting that it was **not** necessary for a patient to understand the cause of a problem to overcome it. Instead of attempting to eliminate a symptom, Dr. Frankl **encouraged** the patient to act-out the aberrant behavior under certain conditions

For example, as the writer, Norman Lobsenz, reported recently in the *San Jose Mercury News,* 4-year-old Tommy threw temper tantrums when he couldn't have his way. The tantrums became a daily occurrence and neither punishment nor reassurance was effective.

Instead of focusing on getting Tommy to give up tantrums, the therapist told the child that it was fine to have a tantrum–but only in a special "tantrum place" at home. "If you start to have one anywhere else, you must stop and wait until you get home to your tantrum place."

Later, the boy was told that he could have a tantrum within a specific time period of 5 p.m. to 7 p.m. If he felt a tantrum coming on, he had to wait until 5 p.m. The surprising results were that Tommy had only one tantrum; and one week later, he gave up tantrums entirely.

As another example of *Paradoxical Therapy* that seems to contradict "common sense" (another fantasy that we agree to call reality?) was a woman with a hand-washing ritual so severe that her hands were raw because she scrubbed them with soap and water every twenty minutes. The therapeutic directions: "Set your oven-timer at twenty minute intervals and wash every time it buzzes."

A week later, the woman called the therapist to ask permission to set the oven-timer at once an hour because every twenty minutes was "too much trouble." By the following week, the compulsion was erased completely.

Paradoxical therapy, according to practitioners, is effective for insomnia, anorexia, procrastination and agoraphobia (fear of public places). In this brainswitching approach, the therapist plays to the right brain. By the creative programming of symptoms, the intervention is *directly with behavior* rather than indirectly through talking about the problem.

In another dramatic illustration of playing to the

right brain, New York psychiatrist, Allen Fay instructed a patient who was fearful of having a relapse into an emotional crisis, "You can't do it unless we plan it." Opening his appointment book, Dr. Fay asked, "When do you want to have it." The puzzled patient picked a date a month later which was penciled in the appointment book.

When the "relapse date" passed, Dr. Fay called the patient and said, You missed your chance. It's too late now." The patient continued to progress.

Paradoxical therapy, according to Lobsenz, has three features. The first is *prescribing the symptom* which means to instruct the patients to continue doing what they want to get rid of. Turn the involuntary behavior into a voluntary scheduled event. The second feature is *provoking rebellion* as when a child refuses to eat vegetables and the parent responds with, "Of course not. Don't eat your vegetables. You're not old enough." And the third feature is *reframing* to shift the person's perspective from negative to positive as Tom Sawyer did in the whitewashing of a fence. Another feature is the *ordeal* in which the task is more stressful than the symptom as when the woman set her oven-timer every twenty minutes to schedule hand-washing.

SUMMARY

Counseling techniques that ask the client to sit down and talk about troubling issues play to the left brain. For talking therapies (either the client talks as in a *non-directive* approach or the therapist talks in a *directive* approach), the probability of an improvement in behavior is a flip of the coin. That is, there is one chance in two for improvement. These odds can be increased to 8 chances in 10 with brainswitching from the left to the right brain.

The reason that talking therapies rarely work is that they play to the left brain which is dedicated to preserving individuals exactly as they are. The left brain does not like novelty. It does not like change. It is "spooked" by any attempt to alter a person's behavior.

Even casual observation of friends who come for "advice" will demonstrate the powerful presence of the ever-critical left brain. For each suggestion we may offer to solve the problem, the person in trouble seems able effortlessly to refute every idea with ingenious reasons why the proposal won't work or can't be implemented.

When counseling plays to the right brain (the uncritical brain) improvement is possible because this hemisphere is open to novelty. It is willing to take risks because it is not spooked by the unknown.

Examples of right brain counseling are *behavior therapy* with techniques such as flooding and desensitization, and *paradoxical therapy*.

Notes

[1]Wolpe (1973a), Wolpe (1973b), p. 62, Wolpe (1978b), p 209 and Wolpe (1981).

[2]Eysenck, 1952, Gelder and Marks (1966), and Paul (1969).

[3]Wolpe (1978a), (1978b).

[4]Marks (In Behavior Modification, W. S. Agras, ed.) 1972. *Note.*–M.A. were not the actual initials of the individual treated.

[5]*Ibid,* p. 186-7.

[6]Marks (1972), p. 187.

[7]*Ibid*, p 197. Note.–B.L. were not the actual initials of the individual in this case.

[8]Marks (1972), p. 197.

[9]*Ibid*, p. 197.

[10]Janet (1925).

[11]Rachman, *et al* (1971).

[12]Case reported in Marks (1972), p. 201. Note–R.M. were not the actual initials of the person treated.

[13]Ibid, p. 202.

[14]Paul (1969). In Behavior Therapy: Appraisal and Status (C.M. Franks, ed.).

[15]Ibid p.117.

[16]Paul (1969), p. 158-9.

[17]DiLoreto (1971).

REFERENCES

DiLoreto, A. O. *Comparative Psychotherapy: An Experimental Analysis*. Chicago: Aldine-Atherton, 1971.

Eyseneck, H. J. The effects of psychotherapy: An evaluation. *J. Consult. Psychol.*, 1952, 16: 319.

Fay, A. *Making Things Better by Making Them Worse.*, (*in press*).

Gelder, M. G., and I. M. Marks. Severe agoraphobia: A controlled prospective trail of behavior therapy. *Brit. J. Psychiat.*, 1966, 112: 309-319.

Janet, P. *Psychological Healing*, Vol. II. New York: Macmillan, 1925.

Lazarus, A., and Fay, A. *I can if I want to*. New York: Warner Books, Inc., 1977.

Lobesenz, N. Don't eat those peas! *Parade Magazine*, page 26-27, San Jose Mercury News, November 22, 1987.

Marks, I. M. Flooding (Implosion) and allied treatments. *In Behavior Modification: Principles and Clinical Applications*. W. S. Agras, ed. Boston: Little, Brown and Company: 151-213, 1972.

Paul, G. L. Outcome of systematic desensitization . . . *In Behavior Therapy: Appraisal and Status*. C.M. Franks, ed. New York: McGraw-Hill Book Co., 63-159, 1969.

Rachman, S., R. Hodgson, and I. M. Marks. Treatment of Chronic Obsessive-Compulsive Neurosis. *Behavior Research and Therapy, 1971,* 9: 237.

Wolpe, J. Evaluation of behavior therapy. Chapter XIV in *The Practice of Behavior Therapy* (2nd ed.). New York: Pergamon Press, 1973a.

Wolpe, J. My philosophy of psychotherapy. J. *of Contemporary Psychotherapy,* 1973b 6(2): 52-62.

Wolpe, J. Cognition and causation in human behavior and its therapy. American *Psychologist,* 1978a 33(5): 437-446.

Wolpe, J. The humanity of behavior therapy. J Behav. *Ther. and Exp. Psychiat.,* 1978b, 9: 205-209. Wolpe, J. Behavior therapy versus psychoanalysis. "American *Psychologist, 1981, 36*(2): 159-164.

CHAPTER 6

THE SELECTION INTERVIEW

THE ILLUSION OF FALSE INFORMATION FROM THE RIGHT BRAIN

In personnel psychology, there is no more baffling phenomenon than the selection interview. If you ask people working in personnel work, "Tell me, why do you interview applicants before deciding whether to hire them?" the typical answers are, ". . . to determine their motivation . . . to evaluate their attitudes . . . to see what they look like . . . to see how they match up in-person with what they submit on paper...to find out how well the applicant will fit in with our organization." The intent, in other words, is to gather information in the interview that is *unique* (could not be obtained in any other way) and use the information to make an accurate selection decision.

Information from the interview is used to forecast how successfully the applicant will perform in the work for which the person is being hired. The key word is, *forecast*. The key thought is that from the interview, we attempt to *predict* future performance of an individual in a specific work situation.

The *interview* is an example of a brainswitch from the left to the right brain. Information plays to the left brain when we see the applicant presented on paper such as the resume, the application form, letters of reference, and paper-and-pencil tests. In the interview, you have a face-to-face contact with the applicant which is input for the right brain. Information in *print* about the applicant plays to the left brain and information from the applicant in a *face-to-face personal interview* plays to the right brain.

The paradox

When personnel managers in 100 companies were asked in a survey, "Of all possible sources of information about an applicant, which do you have the most confidence will accurately predict the person's work behavior for a job?" The sources of information from which the personnel managers had to choose from were the resume, the application form, letters of reference, paper-and-pencil tests, and the selection interview. More than 90% of the personnel managers said that they had the *most confidence* in the interview (Munday, 1968).

If personnel managers had to select only one source of information for making a hiring decision, that would be the interview. The interview inspires the most confidence from people who hire other people.

The puzzle is this: When scholars reviewed research studies of the interview conducted in the past seventy five years, the conclusion from hundreds of studies in a myriad of organizations is that of all possible sources of information about an applicant, **the interview is the least accurate** in forecasting how an applicant will perform on a job for which the person is being hired (Wagner, 1949; England and Paterson, 1960; Mayfield, 1964; Ulrich and Trumbo, 1965; Wright, 1964; and Schmitt, 1976.)

What makes the interview inaccurate is that people who conduct the interviews cannot agree in their evaluations of the applicants. When two people independently interview applicants and the decisions from the interviewers are contradictory, this is like two carpenters measuring a board and one concludes that the board is 3 feet and 5 inches while the other says that the board is 4 feet and 2 inches. Obviously, no cut should be made in the board until both carpenters agree on the measurement.

Unless both interviewers agree, no decision should be made to hire or not to hire. Yet, every day, several hundred thousand people are hired or not hired based upon inaccurate information obtained in the employment interview.

The lack of agreement between interviewers is so serious and shows up in almost every study ever done of the employment interview that researchers England and Paterson from the University of Minnesota recommend that there should be". . . a moratorium on books, articles and other writings about 'how to interview,' 'do's and don'ts' about interviewing, and the like, until there is sufficient research evidence about the reliability and validity of the interview as an assessment device to warrant its use in such work" (p. 62).

Why false confidence in information from the right brain

There are two hypotheses I will present to explain the confidence that personnel people have in the power of interview information to predict work behavior. The first hypothesis is what I call the *Good Judge of Character Illusion.* Every one of us, (but especially personnel people,) believe that we are good judges of character. The belief is so strong that no amount of contradictory evidence will neutralize it. We all feel that if we only meet someone face-to-face, we can "read" the person. We will know what they are about. We can make some accurate predictions about their behavior.

Is that deep-down feeling that we can judge character an illusion? Consider this evidence: Courting is one of the longest interviews ever conducted. A couple seeing each other on dates, conduct a series of interviews for days, weeks, months, even years in which a vast spectrum of information is exchanged. There may be no more thorough and prolonged selection interview than courting. Yet, the probability of successfully selecting a mate in this culture is only one chance in two. In other words, the odds of making an accurate selection decision based on the interview are no better than flipping a coin.

The Good Judge of Character illusion can be seen in medicine. Clinical physicians feel that they are accurate diagnosticians. The feeling seems to be that, "If I can personally examine the person, I can discern what the problem is." There is a strong belief that face-to-face contact between the patient and physician will reveal an accurate diagnosis. This may be an illusion as suggested by two pieces of evidence. The first is that of all sources of information available to a physician for making a diagnosis, the most valuable is a thorough medical history. Secondly, the *New England Journal of Medicine* published a study showing that given a malady with an unknown origin, the probability of an accurate diagnosis from the average physician is only one chance in five (Gross, 1966).

The second hypothesis that could explain the extraordinary confidence that we have in the accuracy of information obtained in the interview is what I call, **The Magic Illusion.** One example of magic is the dictum of veteran politicians that, "If you want to get elected for any political office from dog catcher to President of the United States, get out and shake the hand of every person in your constituency."

Hand-shaking by politicians is so common and well-known that we rarely question the phenomenon. But if you think about it, we seem to be receptive to giving our vote to the candidate who shakes our hand, especially if we have no face-to-face contact with the other candidate. That fleeting touching of the flesh in a hand-shake somehow gives us a feeling of "knowing" the candidate. Somehow the hand-shake inspires confidence.

Another example of magic is our relationship with celebrities. Collecting autographs is magical behavior. Having our picture taken with a celebrity is magical behavior. These artifacts are evidence that we have had face-to-face contact with the celebrity and hence, we know more about that person than someone who has only information from print or the media.

As an extreme example of magical behavior in collecting artifacts of celebrities, there was a photograph years ago on the front page of the *San Francisco Chronicle* showing teen-aged girls eating the grass that the Beatles had stepped on. And, in a follow-up story, the newspaper reported that each item in the wastebasket of the hotel room in which the musicians were staying, was sold for a handsome sum. Even the sheets on which the Beatles slept were cut up into small squares and auctioned off.

Strategies for increasing the reliability of the interview

Before information from the interview can be used to forecast future behavior accurately, the information must be reliable. For the interview, this means that if two or more interviewers talk independently with an interviewee, the final decision to select or not select the candidate will be the same. Reliability means that if we measure the dimensions of a target let us say, the top of a table and then measure the table top again, both measures will give an identical reading.

Consistency of a measurement is absolutely essential before anything else can be done with the information. No arithmetic, for example, can be performed with any measurement that is not reliable because 2 + 2 will not equal 4.

Structure. One strategy that has been suggested in all books in personnel psychology for increasing reliability is to structure the interview. The recommendation is to preplan the interview with a standard series of questions you will ask all interviewees.

This recommendation is based upon several studies which I will review next. The first is a classic study by McMurray in 1947 with a structured interview that he called, the "patterned" interview. The patterned interview involves training the interviewers, having a clear-cut job description, asking identical questions of each interviewee, and at the climax of the interview, making a decision with 1 meaning the applicant is *outstanding*, 2 means the applicant is *good*, 3 is *average* and 4 is *poor*. Before the interview, McMurray had each interviewer call former employers of the applicants and ask a series of questions about the person's work performance.

The patterned interview was tested in three different companies with spectacular results since the validity coefficients were .50 or higher. (A validity coefficient is a index of how accurately the interview information was in forecasting the future work performance of the applicants. Generally, in practical on-the-job situations, .50 or high is considered excellent.) Since the results were consistent in all three organizations, it was assumed that the reliability of the interview was also high.

The problem with the famous McMurray study was this: You will recall that before the interview, each interviewer telephoned former employers and gathered vast information about the applicant's work behavior on previous jobs. This pre-interview information rather than the interview itself probably accounts for the accuracy obtained in McMurray's study since evidence from later studies by Ghiselli, 1966; Asher, 1972 and others suggests that historical data concerning applicants is usually the most accurate in forecasting future job performance of applicants.

In 1969, researchers Schwab and Henneman, III conducted a well-controlled study of *structured* interviews with women who role played being applicants for clerical-stenographic jobs. Interviewers were divided into three groups.

One group of interviewers asked questions spontaneously during the interview in a free, unrestricted manner (called the *unstructured interview*); another group of interviewers read the exact questions on the application form but could follow up with other questions that seemed relevant (this was called the *semi-structured interview*); and the last group of interviewers read the exact questions on the application form but were not permitted to follow-up with further questions (this was the *structured interview*).

The results were that the *unstructured interviews* and the *semi-structured interviews* were unreliable. Only the *structured interview* had acceptable reliability — that is, there was agreement between the interviewers. Again, this study was flawed, in my opinion, because the people conducting the structured interviews were restricted to reading the **exact questions** printed on the application form — and could ask nothing more. This was an orally-administered application form rather than an interview which assumes some **spontaneous interaction** between the interviewer and the person being interviewed.

To resolve the issue, Dr. Milton Hakel of Ohio State University designed the following study: Nine interviewers on a selection board for nurses were asked to use in their inquiry of applicants, a *structured interview* which consisted of a standardized series of questions — meaning that each applicant was asked the identical questions. However, the nine interviewers were encouraged to *probe further* by spontaneously asking *follow-up questions* based upon the answers given by the applicants.

At the climax of an interview, each interviewer made a decision using a sophisticated, state-of-the-art rating called the behaviorally-anchored scale. Even under these optimal conditions, the average agreement between interviewers using a *structured interview* was in the *unreliable* range.

I can only conclude that the recommendation for increasing the reliability of the interview by structuring it (that is, all interviewees are asked the **identical** set of questions), may be a myth. Certainly, the evidence does not support the structured interview as a solution for achieving reliable selection interviews.

After 75 years of research, the problem of how to make the interview a reliable source of information remains one of the great unsolved problems in personnel psychology. In attempting a breakthrough to a solution, Dr. E. C. Webster from McGill University in Canada suggested that clues may be obtained by exploring the factors that influence how interviewers make their decisions. He showed, for example, that when the interviewers read information that applicants had written on the application form **before** the interview, the outcome of the interview could be predicted by the impression from the application form in almost all cases.

In other words, information on the application form accounted for the interviewer's decision to hire or not hire with the experience of the face-to-face interview having almost zero influence. The mystery continues — if the interview does not count in the hiring decisions of the interviewers, then why bother to interview?

A solution: The Q by Q Interview

The solution I am presenting in this chapter is based on the premise that even a brief selection interview of only five to ten minutes is too much information for an interviewer to process with reliability.

The concept, as illustrated in Figure 18, shows that in the traditional interview on the left, the array of data elicited from a respondent in the interview can be organized into a multitude of figure-ground patterns. Each inner circle represents a different interviewer's perception of the information that is seen as important.

The inner circle is figure while the residual, outside the individual's circle, is ground.

TRADITIONAL INTERVIEW
APPROACH

Q BY Q INTERVIEW

Each Rater Selects Information
From a Different Part Of The Field

All Raters Process Information
In Each Part Of The Field

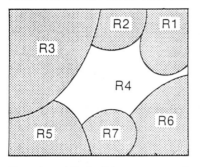

Informational Field	
ALL RATERS
ALL RATERS
ALL RATERS
ALL RATERS
ALL RATERS
ALL RATERS

Result: High Disagreement
Among Raters

Result: High Agreement
Among Raters

Figure 18

When a decision such as a rating is made at the end of an interview, the interviewer has many options in organizing the information into a pattern which can be characterized as important-unimportant, relevant-irrelevant, or predictive-nonpredictive. Since there are many figure-ground options even in a short interview, it is not surprising that the result is likely to be low agreement between raters. In Social Psychology this phenomenon has been extensively explored under the topic of "selective perception."

If my model is valid, it follows that if the interviewer attends systematically to **all parts** of the data field, the results should be high agreement between raters because all interviewers will be processing exactly the same information. The format which I call the *Q by Q Interview*, as shown on the right of Figure 18, requires a decision from the rater (that is, the interviewer) **after each response** to a question asked in the interview.

The Q by Q Interview is a question-by-question decision-making strategy that instructs the interviewer to (a) ask a question, either preplanned or spontaneous, (b) listen with complete attention to the applicant's response, then on the basis of *only* that answer, (c) make a selection decision on a three to seven point scale, (d) cover the rating, try to forget what has been said, and (e) focus full attention on the answer to the next question.

The Q by Q Interview has been tested in a range of situations including the prediction of success for (a) trainees in a nursing program, (b) members of student government, (c) freshman camp counselors, and (d) students experiencing their first course in psychology (Asher, 1970). The Q by Q Interview was pilot-tested to predict trainee success at the Defense Language Institute, West Coast in learning second languages such as Arabic, German, Hungarian, Polish, Russian, Turkish, and Vietnamese (Asher, 1971). The approach has been applied to predict individual differences in carpentry skill (Robertson, 1970), the promotion to police sergeant (Hoeschen, 1977) and the assessment of motivation (Sciarrino and Stephens, 1974).

Results. The findings across most of the pilot studies suggested these conclusions: First, there is a difference between *interrater agreement* (that is, agreement between interviewers) and *interrater reliability*. The former can be present without the latter, but the reverse is usually not true.

For example, when applicants uttered **similar answers** to interview questions, they clustered together in the perception of the interviewers. The result was high interrater agreement (that is, high agreement between the interviewers in their evaluation of the applicants) but low interrater reliability.

This sounds like a contradiction, but it works like this: Since the applicants were extremely close to each other in the perception of the interviewers and the Q by Q Interview accurately measured this clustering together of applicants, the statistic, which was correlation, gave a false reading of a spuriously low interrater reliability. This happens when there is, what is called, *range restriction*. That is, when the elements being assessed are close together, there is the risk that the statistic of correlation will register a false reading, which is what happens when applicants utter **similar answers** to interview questions.

When applicants uttered a **diversity of answers** in response to each interview question in the Q by Q Interview, there was no range restriction with the result that the interviewers applying the Q by Q had significantly higher interrater reliabilities when compared with ratings made only at the end of each interview (as is the custom in the traditional interview).

Other research that supports the Q by Q

Applicants for the Canadian Army. In 1963, Rowe designed a study to explore the impact of "category width" on the decision made to accept or not accept "paper and pencil" applicants for the Canadian Army. Here is how he did it: First, he collected several hundred statements that describe characteristics of people applying for enlistment.

A typical statement might be, "is athletic," another might be "graduated from high school," and still another, "enjoys classical music." Then each statement was rated by a group of judges on a 7 point scale from favorable to unfavorable. That is, if a judge read a statement such as, "is athletic" and perceived that characteristic as favorable, then the judge may assign the statement a 5, 6 or a 7; if the trait was perceived by a judge as unfavorable, then the rating would be 3, 2, or 1 depending upon how unfavorable it was viewed. If a judge responded to a characteristic as neither favorable nor unfavorable for an applicant to have, then the rating would be 4.

The next step was to create 100 hypothetical applicants by combining six characteristics from the list of several hundred statements. Then judges were asked to read the six traits for each of the 100 applicants and make a decision to accept or not accept the "person" into the Canadian Army.

Since each piece of information about an "applicant" was evaluated in a Q by Q decision-making format using a 7 point scale from favorable to unfavorable, I expected the results to show that we could *forecast with accuracy* the acceptance or non-acceptance of "applicants" from the Q by Q information. The results supported my expectation since the validity coefficient (which is an index of forecasting accuracy) was an amazing .71. (In most practical situations in which psychologists attempt to predict any facet of human behavior, a validity of .50 is considered excellent.)

The accuracy of forecasters. The following people seem to have great confidence in making decisions from "complex" information: interviewers of applicants applying for work, clinical psychologists trying to identify the etiology of a psychological problem, stockbrokers predicting future directions of the market, and physicians making a diagnosis. Yet, these individuals do **not** show more accuracy than even simple mathematical models. When experts compete with the mathematical models, the models consistently win in both reliability and validity (Slovic, Fischhoff and Lichtenstein, 1977).

In every "intellectual race" between people and the models, the person used a configural information strategy — that is, the interviewer, the clinical psychologist, the stockbroker, and the physician each reviewed all the data available and made a final decision. In no study did the individual make a decision datum by datum which, according to the Q by Q model, should have dramatically increased both interrater reliability and validity (the index of forecasting accuracy).

Twenty years of decision-making research has demonstrated that people do not compete successfully with mathematical models in making decisions from complex information. It is probably not an oversimplification to conclude that when people make a decision from aggregate information, they appear to be somewhat "mentally retarded;" yet — and this is the astonishing paradox — while making those erroneous judgments, the experts making the predictions are overconfident in their decision-making competency.

For example, in a review of decision making published by the *Oxford University Press,* researchers Slovic, Fischhoff, and Lichtenstein concluded that bankers and stockmarket experts were so inaccurate in predicting closing market prices that a "know nothing" random strategy would have been more accurate. Yet, these experts had a high level of confidence in the accuracy of their forecasts (Stael von Holstein, 1972).

A classic illustration of making decisions from aggregate information is the medical doctor. From a multitude of laboratory tests, interviews, and a physical inspection of the patient, how accurate is the physician's judgment? Sanders (1963) reported to the American Public Health Association that only 40 percent of all human ailments are detected by physicians, while 60 percent are missed. Of the ailments found, half are diagnosed in error. Gross (1966) observed in his book, *The Doctors* that "given an unknown ailment in the body of a patient, the chances of the American physician finding it and diagnosing it correctly are one in five." (p.44)

Just as the interviewers of applicants for work are overconfident in their selection decisions which turn out to be no better than the chance flip of a coin, the paradox applies to many other occupations including *military intelligence analysts* (Brown, Kahr, and Peterson, 1974; Wohlstetter, 1974;), *engineers* (Kidd, 1970), *blackjack gamblers* (Bond, 1974), *psychologists* designing experiments (Cohen, 1962; Brewer and Owen, 1973), *medical clinicians* (Zieve, 1966), *consumers* (Slovic, Kunreuther and White, 1974), *radiologists* (Slovic, *et al.,* 1977) and *financial analysts* (Climo, 1975).

How to increase the accuracy of prediction. Slovic and his colleagues (1977) suggested that a "decomposition" approach is a constructive response to the problem of cognitive overload" (p.17). That is, fractionate the total problem into a series of related parts; then ask the decision-maker to make subjective assessments for **only the smallest components.** This is in harmony with the Q by Q informational model that has been suggested as an aid to decision-making in the selection interview. Notice that both the decomposition approach* and the Q by Q recommend a brainswitch of information from the right to the left brain.

Decision-making and brainswitching

The Q by Q interview may be viewed as a specific application of a larger body of decision-making research which indicates that the optimal aid to human decisions is to decompose aggregate information into subparts, each of which is considered independently. How is this related to the research concerning the right and left brain?

Aggregate information such as the information gathered from an interviewee is input for the right brain because it is configural, experiential, and patterned. The interviewee, for example, is telling a personal story in bits-and-pieces of story-telling that plays to the right brain.

The interviewer is listening with the right brain to information about the interviewee, but at the climax of the interview, the interviewer is asked to make an evaluation which is a brainswitch to the left brain.

Actually, throughout the interview, there is brainswitching back and forth from the right to the left since there is a continual attempt to evaluate incoming

*Research showing that decomposition **improves judgment** has been reported by the following researchers: Armstrong, Denniston and Gordon (1975), Getty, Kelly, and Peterson (1973), Edwards (1962, 1972), Miller, Kaplan, and Edwards (1967, 1969), and Kaplan and Newman (1966).

data. The problem is that the brainswitch is not efficient because every piece of information is not processed.

The right brain accepts input flowing in rapidly as one pattern follows another, but the left brain prefers a systematic, sequential series of small inputs. Hence, there is **conflict** between the hemispheres. Also, the right brain accepts the input on face value while the left tries in vain to scan the fast-moving display of complex, patterned information in an attempt to evaluate it. The right brain is letting information flow in and then flashing it to the left brain for evaluation, but it is coming too fast and in too much volume for the left brain to scan with a thorough and systematic evaluation. Not only is the information coming to the left brain rapidly and in heavy volume, but the format of the input is alien to the left brain since it is a convoluted, stream of fragmented patterns.

The result is that the left brain does the best it can do to handle the **overload** which is transmitted by the right brain in a format that is incompatible with left brain input, but only bits-and-pieces can be selected for examination. *Most of the transmission from the right brain is unprocessed by the left brain.*

Hence, most of the information from the interview is wasted. It is not an unreasonable hypothesis that the left brain may be almost randomly selecting from the complex stream of fast-moving patterns that are coming in. In any event, only a tiny portion of the interview data are processed by the left brain. For example, Webster found in twenty Canadian companies, that after only *four minutes,* on the average, interviewers feel that they have enough information to make a decision to hire or not to hire.

To compensate for the handicap that the left brain has in receiving information from the interview, a decomposition information processing strategy such as the Q by Q model is critical for the optimal power of the left brain to evaluate, with accuracy, incoming information.

SUMMARY

Information gathered in face-to-face contact between people plays to the right brain. Since the right brain is uncritical, it must flash incoming information to the left brain for evaluation.

The problem is that the brainswitching from right to left is too fast and too convoluted in complex patterns for the left brain to process thoroughly. The speed and texture of the data from the right brain are difficult for the left brain to scan systematically and carefully. Hence, only tiny bits-and-pieces are selected for evaluation.

Since each interviewer is selecting a different array of bits-and-pieces from the voluminous flow of patterns flooding in from the right to the left brain, it is not surprising that interviewers do not agree in their decision-making. A solution is a style of information processing in which the answer to each question from a respondent is evaluated by the left brain; then the left brain is asked to focus full attention on the answer to the next question and make a decision, etc.

The result is that every bit of information from a respondent is evaluated by each interviewer and hence, there is agreement in their final decision-making. The name I have given this information processing strategy is the **Q by Q Interview.**

The false confidence that personnel people and others have in the usual selection interview comes, I believe, from the fact that face-to-face contact plays to the right brain which is uncritical of its own performance. Furthermore, the selection interview is the preferred source of information about applicants because it is perceived as play.

Since the interview is right brain input, it is more relaxing and enjoyable than reading information in print about the applicant or evaluating paper-and-pencil data from tests. Reading about the applicant and evaluating test data are left brain input which is in the zone of work and also becomes the target of intense critical activity.

REFERENCES

Armstrong, J. S., Denniston, W. B., Jr., & Gordon, M. M. The use of the decomposition principle in making judgments. *Organizational Behavior and Human Performance,* 1975, *14,* 257-263.

Arvey, R. D. Unfair discrimination in the employment interview: Legal and psychological aspects. *Psychology Bulletin,* 1979, *86*(4), 736-765.

Asher, J. J. How the applicant's appearance affects the reliability and validity of the interview. *Educational and Psychological Measurement,* 1970, *30,* 687-695.

Asher, J. J. Q by Q interview as a predictor of success in second language learning. *Psychological Reports,* 1971, *29,* 331-337.

Asher, J. J. The biographical item: Can it be improved? *Personnel Psychology,* 1972, *25,* 251-269.

Bernstein, V., Hakel, M. D., & Harlan, A. The college student as interviewer: A threat to generalizability? *Journal of Applied Psychology,* 1975, *60,* 266-268.

Bond, N. A., Jr. Basic strategy and expectation in casino blackjack. *Organizational Behavior and Human Performance,* 1974, *12,* 413-428.

Brewer, J. K., & Owen, P. W. A note on the power of statistical tests. *Journal of Educational Measurement,* 1973, *10,* 71-74.

Brown, R. V., Kahr, A. S., & Peterson, C. *Decision analysis for the manager.* New York: Holt, Reinhart & Winston, 1974.

Climo, T. A. Cash flow statements for investors. Unpublished, University of Kent at Canterbury, 1975.

Cohen, J. The statistical power of abnormal-social psychological research. *Journal of Abnormal and Social Psychology,* 1962, *65,* 145-153.

Dipboye, R. L., & Wiley, J. W. Reactions of male raters to interviewee self-presentation style and sex: Extensions of previous research. *Journal of Vocational Behavior,* 1978, *13,* 192-203.

Edwards, W. Dynamic decision theory and probabilistic information processing. *Human Factors,* 1962, *4,* 59-73.

Edwards, W. Application of research on cognition to man-machine system design. Engineering Psychology Lab. Reports, 010342-1-F. Ann Arbor: University of Michigan, 1972.

Edwards, W., John, R. S., & Stillwell, W. Final research report: Research on the technology of inference and decision. (SSRI Research Report 79-1). Los Angeles: University of Southern California, Social Science Research Institute, January 1979.

England, G. W., & Paterson, D. G. Selection and placement—the past ten years. In H. G. Heneman, Jr., L. C. Brown, M. K. Chandler, R. Kahn, H. S. Parnos, & G. P Schultz (eds.), *Employment relations research*. New York: Harper, 1960.

Gettys, C. F., Kelly, C. W. III, & Peterson, C. R. The best guess hypothesis in multistage inference. *Organizational Behavior and Human Performance,* 1973, *10,* 354-373.

Ghiselli, E. E. *The validity of occupational aptitude tests.* New York: John Wiley, 1966.

Goldberg, L. R. Diagnosticians vs. diagnostic signs: The diagnosis of psychosis vs. neurosis from the MMPI. *Psychological Monographs*, 1965, 79, (9, Whole No. 602).

Goldberg, L. R. Simple models or simple processes? Some research on clinical judgments. *American Psychologist*, 1968, *23,* 483-496..

Goldberg, L. R. The search for configural relationships in personality assessment: The diagnosis of psychosis vs. neurosis from the MMPI. *Multivariate Behavioral Research,* 1969, *4,* 523-536.

Goldberg, L. R., Man versus model of man: A rationale, plus some evidence, for a method of improving on clinical inferences. *Psychological Bulletin*, 1970, *73,* 422-432.

Gross, M. L. *The doctors*. New York: Dell Publishing Company, 1966.

Hakel, M. D., Hollmann, T. D., & Dunnette, M. D. Accuracy of interviewers, certified public accountants, and students in identifying the interests of accountants. *Journal of Applied Psychology*, 1970, *54*, 115-119. (a)

Hakel, M. D., Ohnesorge, J. P., & Dunnette, M. D. Interviewer evaluations of job applicants' resumes as a function of the qualifications of the immediately preceding applicants: An examination of contrast effects. *Journal of Applied Psychology*, 1970, *54,* 27-30. (b)

Hakel, M. D. Similarity of post-interview trait rating intercorrelations as a contributor to interrater agreement in a structured employment interview. *Journal of Applied Psychology,* 1971, *55*(5), 443-448.

Hamner, W. C., Kim, J. S., Baird, L., & Bigoness, W. J. Race and sex as determinants of ratings by potential employers in a simulated work-sampling task. *Journal of Applied Psychology*, 1974, *59*, 497-499.

Heneman, H. G. III. Impact of test information and applicant sex on applicant evaluations in a selection simulation. *Journal of Applied Psychology*, 1977, *62*(4), 524-526.

Hoeschen, P. L. Using the Q by Q interview to predict success as a police sergeant. Unpublished master's thesis, San Jose State University, 1977.

Imada, A. S., & Hakel, M. D. Influence of nonverbal communication and rater proximity on impressions and decisions in simulated employment interviews. *Journal of Applied Psychology,* 1977, *62*(3), 295-300.

Kaplan, R. J., & Newman, J. R. Studies in probabilistic information processing. *IEEE Transactions on Human Factors in Electronics,* 1966, *Hfe-7*(1), March, 49-63.

Kidd, J. B. The utilization of subjective probabilities in production planning. *Acta Psychol.,* 1970, *34,* 338-347.

London, M., & Hakel, M. D. Effects of applicant stereotypes, order, and information on interview impressions. *Journal of Applied Psychology,* 1974, *59*(2), 157-162.

Mayfield, E. C. The selection interview—A re-evaluation of published research. *Personnel Psychology,* 1964, *17,* 239-250.

McGee, R. K. Response style as a personality variable: By what criterion? *Psychological Bulletin,* 1962, *59,* 284-295.

McMurray, R. N. Validating the patterned interview. *Personnel,* 1947, 23, 2-11.

Meehl, P. E. *Clinical versus statistical prediction: A theoretical analysis and a review of the evidence.* Minneapolis: University of Minnesota Press, 1954.

Meehl, P. E. A comparison of clinicians with five statistical methods of identifying psychotic MMPI profiles. *Journal of Counseling Psychology,* 1959, *6,* 102-109.

Miller, L. W., Kaplan, R. J. & Edwards, W. Judge: A value-judgment-based tactical command system. *Organizational Behavior and Human Performance,* 1967, *2*(4), 239-374.

Miller, L. W., Kaplan, R. J., & Edwards, W. Judge: A laboratory evaluation. *Organizational Behavior and Human Performance,* 1969, *4*(2), 97-111.

Munday, P. A. A study on the use of the interview in 42 large companies in three Bay Area counties. Unpublished student project, San Jose State University, San Jose, CA, May, 1968.

Robertson, B. R. An assessment of the Q by Q interview technique. Unpublished master's thesis, San Jose State University, 1970.

Rosen, B., & Jerdee, T. H. Influence of sex role stereotypes on personnel decisions. *Journal of Applied Psychology.* 1974, *59*(1), 9-14.

Rosen, B., & Jerdee, T. H. The nature of job-related age stereotypes. *Journal of Applied Psychology,* 1976, *61*(2), 180-183. (a)

Rosen, B., & Jerdee, T. H. The influence of age stereotypes on managerial decisions. *Journal of Applied Psychology,* 1976, *61*(4), 428-432. (b)

Rowe, P. M. Individual differences in selection decisions, *Journal of Applied Psychology,* 1963, *47*(5), 304-307.

Sanders, B. S. Completeness and reliability of diagnosis in therapeutic practice. Paper presented at the statistics section of the American Public Health Association meetings, November 14, 1963.

Schmitt, N. Social and situational determinants of interview decisions: Implications for the employment interview. *Personnel Psychology,* 1976, *29*, 79-101.

Schwab, D. P., & Heneman, H. C., III. Relationship between interview structure and inter-interviewer reliability in an employment situation. *Journal of Applied Psychology*, 1969, *53*, 214-217.

Sciarrino, J. A. & Stephens, R. N. The assessment of motivation with the Q by Q interview technique, Unpublished master's thesis, San Jose State University, 1974.

Seaver, D. A., Assessment of group preference and group uncertainty for decision making (SSRI Tech. Report, 76-4). Los Angeles: University of Southern California, Social Science Research Institute, June, 1976.

Shaw, E. A. Differential impact of negative stereotyping in employee selection. *Personnel Psychology*, 1972, *25*, 333-338.

Slovic, P., Fischhoff, B., & Lichtenstein, S. Behavioral decision theory. *Annual Review of Psychology*, 1977, *28*, 1-40.

Slovic, P., Kunreuther, H., & White, G. F. Decision processes, rationality and adjustment to natural hazards. In G. F. White (ed.), *Natural hazards, local, national and global*. New York: Oxford University Press, 1974.

Stael von Holstein, C. A. S. Probalistic forecasting: An experiment related to the stock market. *Organizational Behavior and Human Performance*, 1971, *8*, 139-168.

Ulrich, L., & Trumbo, D. The selection interview since 1949. *Psychological Bulletin*, 1965, *63*, 100-116.

Wagner, R. The employment interview: A critical summary. *Personnel Psychology*, 1949, *2*, 17-46.

Washburn, P. V., & Hakel. M. D. Visual cues and verbal content as influences on impressions formed after simulated employment interviews. *Journal of Applied Psychology,* 1973, *58*(1), 137-141.

Webster, E. C. *Decision making in the employment interview.* Montreal: McGill University, 1964.

Wexley, K. N., & Nemeroff, W. F. The effects of racial prejudice, race of applicant, and biographical similarity on interviewer evaluations of job applicants. *Journal of Social and Behavioral Sciences*, 1974, *20,* 66-78.

Wexley, K. N., Sanders, R. E., & Yukl, G. A. Training interviewers to eliminate contrast effects in employment interviews. *Journal of Applied Psychology*, 1973, *57*(3), 233-236.

Wexley, K. N., Yukl, G. A., Kovacs, S. Z., & Sanders, R. E. Importance of contrast effects in employment interviews. *Journal of Applied Psychology,* 1972, *56,* (1), 45-48.

Wohlstetter, A. Legends of the strategic arms race, Part I: The driving machine. *Strategic Review,* 1974, 67-92.

Wright, O. R., Jr. Summary of research on the selection interview since 1964. *Personnel Psychology*, 1969, *22*, 391-413.

Zieve, L. Misinterpretation and abuse of laboratory tests by clinicians. *Annals of the New York Academy of Science,* 1966, *134*, 563-572.

CHAPTER 7

PROBLEM SOLVING

THE PROBLEM IS: WHAT IS THE PROBLEM?

Books on problem solving assume that the problem is obvious. Usually, it is not.

Notice in those books written to enhance one's problem solving skills, the "problem" is a "given" and the solution is the unknown in the equation. This is Aristotelian two-valued logic with a problem and a solution in which the former is known and the latter unknown. These categories are presented as an either-or situation in which the problem is "bad" and the solution is "good."

The truth is that few things are in either-or categories. For example, sex is not categorical. Biologically and chemically, we are not male or female, but somewhere on a continuum between the two poles. Even death is not categorical. There is quite a controversy in medicine as to when someone is dead. Further, different parts of the body seem to die at different times. This perplexity about when someone is "pronounced" dead — and notice that the word "pronounced" implies an opinion, not a fact — is extremely important because it guides the decision to remove body parts for transplant to others.

What I will demonstrate later in this chapter is that the very creation and use of a category called a "problem" and another category called a "solution" complicates the process of problem solving. More about this later.

Why problems are not puzzles

Problems are often confused with puzzles. They are not the same. For example, here is a **puzzle**, but not a genuine problem: At sunrise one morning, a monk begins to climb a tall mountain. The monk ascends the spiraling path pausing many times to rest. He reaches the top before sunset and after several days of meditation, he starts down again at sunrise. Prove that there is a spot along the path that the monk will occupy at precisely the same time of the day on both trips.

The monk's journey is a puzzle rather than a genuine problem for two reasons. First, it is of peripheral interest since most people "do not care." Secondly, it is trivial because at least one solution is known before the question was asked.

The monk puzzle is like the word problems in algebra books. For example, Ellen is 7 years older than her sister, and the sum of their ages is 21 years. How old is each?

There are many irrationalities in so-called algebraic word problems. For instance, they are puzzles, not problems because no one cares one way or the other about Ellen or her sister. The situation is nonsensical. I challenge anyone to find one — only one — meaningful, genuine word problem in any algebra book. There are none.

Also, not only is the answer already known, but the answer came before the question. In other words, before a question can be asked about the ages of Ellen and her sister in the manner it was asked, the ages of both people had to be known in advance. So why ask the question?

If you are skeptical that the question always follows the answer in those algebraic word puzzles, consider this: Unless you already know the ages of both Ellen and her sister how can you conclude (a) that Ellen is 7 years older than her sister, and (b) the sum of their ages is 21 years?

In this next example taken from a textbook used in the first course in algebra, the author had to know the "unknowns" in order to ask the question. The question, incidentally, will be of no interest to anyone — not even the author of the algebra text: "In a class of 37 pupils there are 5 more girls than boys. How many boys and how many girls are there?"

Another irrationality of the algebraic word puzzles is that they are presented "to increase the student's problem solving skills." Nonsense. There has never been demonstrated in any study that practice in "solving" algebraic word puzzles will transfer to any other type of problem solving — quantitative or verbal. Solving those puzzles simply makes one more proficient at solving other puzzles just as trivial.

If problems are not puzzles and problems are not in a category that is the opposite of solutions, then what are problems? How should they be conceptualized?

Let's start with this concept: The steady state is that everything — persons, places, animals, things, events — all are imperfect. That is a given. (The only exception may be Euclid's geometry in which the geometrical relationships fit together so perfectly that when Einstein, as a boy, first opened Euclid's book* which some-

---

*Incidentally, Euclid's book is the second best-selling book on record, exceeded only by the Bible.

one had given him as a gift, he was thrilled because he felt that this was the only experience he had of perfection and therefore, the book must be a glimpse into the working of the Divine Mind.)

Imperfection is on a continuum from small to large, microscopic to visible-with-the-naked-eye. Imperfections are not only of different magnitudes, but they tend to be in motion. They are expanding or contracting in size. The velocity of movement is also on a continuum from slow to fast.

Any event, for example, is imperfect with flaws that may be small or large, expanding or contracting. Usually, we will only label the flaw as a problem when it has expanded to a size that produces feelings of discomfort, irritation, or tension. We could conceptualize the continuum of changing imperfection as being located some place in these zones: Imagine on the left, a **green zone** in which the size of the flaw is imperceptible. Adjacent is a **yellow zone** in which the flaw has now become large enough to be noticeable but only mildly disturbing. Finally, on the right, picture a **red zone** in which the imperfection is large enough to generate tension. Once in the red zone, there is enough stress to produce a response such as, "We have a problem. Something must be done about it."

Once the imperfection is in the red zone, there is motivation to transform — that is, alter the event in some way that will contract the size of the imperfection to move us back into the green zone. This alteration we call "a solution."

SOME EXAMPLES

Ordinary drinking water is a classic example of an imperfection moving from the green zone into the yellow zone and then into the red zone. Writer-scholars such as Rachel Carson warned us years ago about the threat to clean drinking water from pesticides. At that time, the imperfection was imperceptible and hence in the green zone. Gradually, the imperfection expanded in size, passing from the yellow to the red zone. The flaw now is so acute in some communities that there is no public drinking water that can be consumed safely.

The dependency upon chemistry such as pesticides to "solve problems" prompted the publisher of *Organic Gardening and Farming* to write warning editorials for the past 30 years about the depletion in the soil of trace elements such as zinc and magnesium. This deficit seems to be a consequence of reliance on chemical fertilizers instead of replenishing the soil with humus. In the old days, family farmers would continually plow under humus in the form of animal waste, composted garbage, and cover crops of legumes. The imperfection of non-replenishment of the soil has moved to the yellow zone with more people aware but only mildly concerned. The connection between soil chemistry and health is still rather vague in the public mind.

The "problem" of human waste is another interesting example. There are two flaws in our disposal of human waste: First, precious water is wasted in the flushing procedure and the second is that we don't know what to do with the solid waste. Both flaws have entered the red zone in many communities.

The publisher I have just quoted has suggested for

many years that "human waste" has been misperceived. We are dealing not with waste, but a valuable source of humus which our soil desperately needs, to produce healthy crops. This has been demonstrated in China for hundreds of years. The answer, according to publisher Rodale, is to process the "waste" to produce sludge which can be used as a safe organic fertilizer. Following Rodale's argument to a logical conclusion, perhaps the best gift we can give to future generations is to bury our biodegradable garbage in our backyards.

Incidentally, the most important function of scholar-writers is to alert us about the expansion rate of flaws so that we can anticipate when a flaw will enter the red zone. This means, of course, that we will have lead time to create modifications (to alter events) that will reverse the direction of the flaw to move it back into the green zone.

From the examples I have presented, it appears that flaws expand from left to right as they go from the green to the yellow to the red zone in an orderly linear progression. Not necessarily.

A flaw can be in the green zone and instantly move in a flash into the red zone. This happens when someone invents an alternate way of doing something. For example, kerosene lamps were in the green zone — that is, for generations the imperfections were imperceptible until Thomas E. Edison created another option, the electric light.

In comparison with the electric light, the kerosene lamp moved immediately from the green into the red zone. Kerosene became an unacceptable source of light for most people. (In the interest of historical accuracy, the electric light was not instantly recognized as a better option. For instance, when electric lights were installed in the grand old Del Coronado Hotel in San Diego, a note was posted in each room with the message: "Please do not try to light with a match. Turn the key. The electric light will not harm your health.")

Another example of a flaw that jumped from the green directly into the red zone was the introduction of jet engines in commercial airlines. The airline companies took a daring chance by investing millions to build the first jet-powered airliners for domestic travel because no one could predict whether consumers would accept the innovation. If consumers rejected the jets in favor of piston-driven aircraft, then the companies had multi-million dollar "white elephants" tethered in their hangars.

Happily, there was instant public acceptance. In comparison with the jets, the imperfections of piston planes expanded suddenly in the perception of the consumer to miserable proportions. The flaws that were in the yellow zone (that is, mildly disturbing) now moved to the red zone (they were intolerable). The flaws: piston planes were often noisy and turbulent, with a high probability of passenger air sickness.

Water-base paints is another example. For generations, only oil-base paints were available. People grumbled about the imperfections including the difficult clean-up, but consumer perception of stress was mild — that is, in the yellow zone. With the introduction of water-base paints, both the application and clean-up were simplified which suddenly moved the perception of imperfections for oil-base paints into the red zone.

BRAINSWITCHING

The green, yellow and red zones are related to brainswitching. For concepts that we have internalized, the left brain produces "concept constancy," which means that imperfections are reduced in magnitude to move us into the green zone. There is resistance from the left brain for any attempt at "concept disruption." The left brain works to preserve existing concepts that the system has already internalized and to magnify imperfections in competing concepts, moving them into the red zone.

The left brain works to keep existing concepts in the green zone and novel concepts in the red zone. The task in problem solving is to "quiet" the left brain to allow the novel concept to be received by the right brain and then accepted by the left brain. The easiest way to "quiet" the left brain is with an invention that demonstrates to the left brain's satisfaction that if the novel concept replaces an existing concept, flaws will be eliminated.

But what happens when no alternatives to existing concepts have been invented? How do we create alternatives when the left brain is working diligently to keep existing concepts in the green zone which means that we have no motivation to search for alternative concepts?

The role of "reality" in solving problems

Once a concept is formed, its existence, like the human body, has an index of health and longevity. The left brain resists the initial formation of concepts because the left brain prefers the familiar; but, once a concept is formed and internalized, the left brain attempts to protect the concept from injury or death.

The left brain prefers to occupy the green zone in which the perception of imperfections are in the periphery of awareness. This is the zone of comfort — perhaps the zone of sanity.

"Reality" is the pictures in our head which we call concepts. We see, hear, smell, and touch not with our eyes, ears, nose, and hands, but with concepts. Without concepts, we would be like Helen Keller before working with her gifted teacher.

Insight into the nature of "reality" can be achieved from the classic studies by M. V. Senden at the University of Berlin in 1932. Adults, blind from birth, had cataracts surgically removed from their eyes and suddenly they were no longer blind. What did they see?

Psychologists were keenly interested in what the adults could see since the information might solve the mystery of what people innately see without learning or language. What are people capable of seeing without learned concepts? The adults in Senden's study were concept-free.

The findings of the Senden studies were so spectacular that I will reenact what happened in detail. Pretend that you are M. V. Senden, a research psychologist examining each patient in the hospital.

You place two objects on the table in front of the patient. You say, "Tell me, what do you see ?"

The patient responds, "I see two of something — two different things."

"Do you know what they are?"

"No."

"Let me tell you — this is an orange and this is a piece of coal. Now, please close your eyes."

You interchange the location of the orange and the piece of coal. Then, you say, "Please open your eyes and tell me which is the orange and which is the piece of coal?"

Amazingly, the patient furrows his brow, and says hesitatingly, "I don't know."

"All right, let's try again. This is the orange and this is the piece of coal."

It took hundreds of trials before a patient could visually differentiate an orange from a piece of coal. Of course, when the patient was invited to touch the objects, there was instant identification with, "Ah, this is the orange and this, of course, is the coal." During the years of sightlessness, this individual had formed tactile concepts. But without visual concepts, the person was genuinely blind even though the individual's eyes were functioning normally.

Even more dramatically, when two people were invited into the room and the examiner said to the patient, "What do you see?" the patient said, "Two of something — probably people."

"Do you see two or just one of something?"

"No, they are different."

"Do you recognize what you are looking at?"

"No."

"Let me give you some hints. You are looking at two people. Now, I want to know whether they are children or adults, males or females — or what?"

"I honestly don't know."

The examiner continued, "Let me give you some clues. This (POINTING TO THE MAN) is a man and this (POINTING TO THE WOMAN) is a woman. They are both adults. Again, this is the man and this is the woman. Please close your eyes."

Both people left the room and the patient was asked to open his eyes. The examiner said, "I'm going to ask each person you just saw to come into the room, one at a time. I would like you to tell me whether you see a man or a woman."

The man entered and the examiner asked, "Is this a man or a woman?"

"I don't know."

Next, the woman entered the room. "Is this a man or a woman?"

"I really don't know."

Of course, when the man or woman spoke, the patient could make an immediate identification of sex. Also, if the patient is permitted to touch the person's face and hair, recognition was instantaneous.

However, it took hundreds of trials before the patient could visually distinguish a man from a woman or an adult from a child.

Conclusion. We see, hear, smell, and touch with concepts and not with our eyes, ears, nose, and hands. Input from the outside world into our sense receptors such as light into our eyes is, without concepts, a confusing and bewildering array of shapes. Even an "obvious," "transparent," and "simple" pattern such as the identification of a *short stick* compared with a *long stick* was "unseen" by the 66 patients studied by researcher Senden.

The patients required hundreds of trials before any could, with consistency, say which of two sticks was longer or shorter. Then, after the exhausting experience of attempting to differentiate which of two objects was longer or taller, if the context was *altered slightly,* the patients became confused and learning seemed to vanish.

We "see" with concepts and not with our eyes. Anyone who has little aptitude or interest in mechanical things will appreciate this example. If the car of an unmechanical person breaks down on the highway, that person can open the hood of the car and peer at the engine, but will see nothing except an alien arrangement of metal fused together in different sizes, shapes, and colors. There will be no inkling of the problem.

Nothing is obvious without concepts — not even which of two sticks is longer or shorter. And once concepts are formed, there is a resistance to extinction. Like people and other living things, concepts seem to have a yearning to continue their existence. This is not anthropomorphic poetry. It has a factual basis which may be critical to solving problems.

The evidence that concepts resist "death"

Once concepts are formed, they resist death. The evidence to support that hypothesis comes from the fascinating work of experimental psychologists working with a phenomenon called, "constancy."

To explain constancy, let us start with this illusion: What we see with our eyes seems to correspond with what is outside of ourselves. Hence, we tend to conclude that our eyes are a sort of "window to the world." Not so. Not so, at all.

For instance, try this demonstration: Prop this book in an upright position on your desk. Then, with your eyes still on the book walk backwards away from the book, pause, and walk towards the book.

What did you see? As you backed away, did the book change in size from a huge object to a speck? As you approached the book, did it suddenly expand from a thimble size to the size of a billboard? As you moved to different positions around the book, did it tilt, yaw, tremble, tip, jump, spin, or shutter?

Probably none of those things happened. As one moves towards or away from the book, it still appears to remain about the same size. It did not zoom from a small to a huge size and back again. It is stable. The shape remains the same. It did not change suddenly from a rectangle to a square to a trapezoid to an ellipse.

All quite ordinary. But, the mystery is this: The image of the book coming into the lens of the viewer's eye produces a kind of "motion picture" on the retina which is the back of the eye. When one stands up and walks away, still looking at the book, the image on the retina did zoom from a large to a small size. Then, as one approaches the book, the size on the retina expands dramatically. There is a distinct change in the size of the retinal image of the book that corresponds to the distance one moves. This is not a tiny, imperceptible change, but a drastic expansion and contraction.

Then, as one moves around the book, the retinal image changes its shape from a rectangle to a square to a trapezoid to an ellipse. Not only was the shape of the book's image changing radically on the retina, but on the back of the eye, the book's image was moving with every slight movement of the viewer's head. For example, the retinal image of the book was tilting, yawing, trembling, tipping, jumping, spinning, and shuttering. Certainly it was not stable and stationary; yet, that is how it appears which is the illusion of "constancy."

Conclusion. Images projected to the back of the eye from the outside are constantly changing in shape and size as the distance and angle of view shift between the observer and external objects. Even though shape and size of retinal images are shifting rapidly and continually, the viewer "sees" objects and people as **stable** in size and shape except for extreme distances. This stability is called "constancy." What is input to the sense receptors of the eyes is not what we see. We convert the sensory input into information (or concepts) that correspond to the "actual" shape and size of entities in the external world.

Senden's sixty-six cataract patients who were blind from birth were without visual concepts when their sight was restored. Hence, when they looked, they only saw the confusing and bewildering array of shapes, sizes, and colors projected on the retina.

The phenomenon of constancy gives us two valuable insights: The first is that input to the sense receptors is converted into information (concepts) which are used to provide the *experience* of seeing, hearing, touching, and smelling. Secondly, and this is my hypothesis, constancy is a function of the left brain. Once the left hemisphere accepts a concept, it has constancy; it has stability; it resists extinction. (It should be noted here that only the right brain internalizes concepts with the left brain accepting or rejecting the incorporation. The more times the left rejects the concept which tentatively resides in the right brain, the more difficulty one will have in recalling the concept.)*

Converting sensory input into information

Information is concepts, and concepts are categories. How much of the input to our sense receptors is converted into categories? The answer is that the more skill one has in the use of a category, the more one has filtered out sensory input. For example, in linguistics, a native speaker with exquisite skill in a language, has filtered out perhaps 99% of auditory input coming into the person's ears. The native speaker is converting only 1% of the input into information and "unlistening" to 99%. The more sophisticated one's skill (i.e., one's application of categories), the smaller the input needed for conversion to categories.

If the example is turned inside-out, the principle of filtering out sensory input from categories may be clearer. In attempting to acquire a second language, the learner has the perception that native speakers are

---

*Elsewhere I have reviewed the evidence for "first" trial" learning. See Asher, 1986, pages 1-7 to 1-14.

talking at machine-gun velocity — so fast that most of what the learner hears is an incomprehensible blur. As the learner's skill with the new language increases, talk from native speakers seems to get slower and slower until finally, the utterances are in slow-motion.

Of course, there is no change in the velocity of speech from native speakers, only the perception of the learner changes. The learner decelerated the rate of talk from native speakers by *unhearing* more and more sensory input that was non-informational. Categories were purged of all sensory input except the minimum necessary to retrieve concepts.

SKILL LEARNING

Skill learning means to filter out of categories all non-informational sensory input. When a category is empty of all sensory input except what is absolutely necessary to retrieve the concept, the concept becomes stable. The end-product of skill learning is concept constancy (CC) while problem solving is the reverse process in which we produce concept disruption (CD). In the former, the left brain has been persuaded to accept a concept and in the latter, the left brain has been persuaded to reject a concept that is already in the system (Asher, 1963).

Human access to sensory input

The more sophisticated we are with the application of categories we have internalized, the less sensory input we need. But, if sensory input is the raw data from which we form concepts, then how much sensory stimulation is available to us? The answer may be surprising.

All energy is on a continuum which we have artificially divided into categories labeled, for example, as "light," "sound," "electricity," "X-ray," and "radar" plus many other categories. Notice that the categories we have created give the illusion that light is different from sound and sound is different from electricity and so forth, but inside the human body, light waves coming into our eyes and sound waves coming into our ears are identical signals. The signals are so indistinguishable that if the neurological wire that usually carries the signal from the eyes to the area of the brain reserved for vision is connected up to the brain location reserved for audition, then we would hear the light coming into our eyes. Likewise, the neurological wire coming from the the ear would enable us to "see" sounds if the wire was connected to the brain location reserved for vision.

There is another peculiar fact (that I mentioned before) which is valuable in problem solving and it is this: If you held in your hands a fishing pole with the line on your reel being the electromagnetic continuum, how far would the line extend out into space if you released the line on the reel? The answer is 300 billion miles*.

The sense receptors on the human body are capable of receiving signals from the electromagnetic continuum — but, we can pick up signals from only one mile on a band of signals that is 300 billion miles long. Only one mile — that's all.

Consider what our "reality" might be if nature had shifted our location on the electromagnetic spectrum just one mile in either direction. Let us say that the shift placed us in the segment called, "X-rays." Then we would probably "see" persons, places, and things as

*Source: Moody Institute film entitled, *Sense Perception: Part II.*

blurred silhouettes in which we would perhaps see blood circulating, food digesting, and the content in the stomach.

Notice that we have a vague concept of X-rays, but no concepts for other parts of the electromagnetic continuum. It seems certain, however, that reality as humans conceive it would be an entirely different experience — completely alien and unrecognizable from our present consciousness.

The experiences of animals and insects are unknown to us because they are receiving signals from a different part of the continuum. For example, dogs can hear signals outside of our range of reception and bats respond to signals in a radar band of the continuum. The reality of insects is baffling to us because we have yet to map the location on the continuum where they receive signals. How, for instance, is a scout ant able to detect a piece of candy in the top drawer of a bureau, climb what must be the sheer cliff of a mountain to verify the prize, then "report" back to the tribe of ants?

SELECTIVE PERCEPTION

Humans occupy only a scratch on the electromagnetic continuum which is like a few grains of sand in the Sahara Desert. But even that minute segment is a vast overestimation since only a small portion of signals in the the human range of reception, is converted into information. Psychologists call it, *selective perception* which means that there is no straight-through-transmission from light coming into the eyes to images in the brain.

Rather, it seems to work like a switchboard at the

White House in Washington, D. C. An incoming call does not immediately ring in the Oval Office of the President. A secretary screens the call and makes a decision such as (a) a staff member should receive this call, or (b) I will write down the message and send a condensation to the President, or (c) the call should be switched to the President.

As I will demonstrate later, selective perception is a powerful problem solving skill. There is abundant evidence from the research by psychologists to support the existence of selective perception. For example, in the research called, "dichotic listening," a person is asked to put on head phones and is then instructed to "shadow your left ear" which means to focus attention only to what is heard with the left ear. Next, a voice on tape utters a message that is transmitted through the head phones to the right ear and simultaneously, a different message is spoken to the left ear.

The results, demonstrated in many experiments, are that a person can voluntarily "unhear" what is being said in the individual's right ear and only "hear" the message being uttered in the left ear. Of course, this works in reverse. One can "shadow" the right ear and "unhear" the message coming into the left ear.

Since the neurological wiring from each ear is crossed in the brain — that is, the left ear is wired to the right hemisphere and the right ear is wired to the left hemisphere, the dichotic listening experiments suggest to me that attention can be shifted voluntarily and instantly from one hemisphere of the brain to the other.

Dichotic listening can be observed at cocktail parties. Even though many conversations are going on simultaneously with different fragments coming into each ear, we are able to hear selectively one conversation and "unhear" the others. The conclusion: Only a small part of the raw data coming into our senses from the tiny, broadcasting band that we can tune into, is processed into information that is transmitted to awareness.

LEFT BRAIN SET

If we can shift the focus of our attention from one hemisphere of the brain to the other, what determines the brainswitch? How do we decide which part of the incoming signals to respond to?

One way we make the decision is called "set." We create a set by creating a goal that produces an expectation of what will happen. For example, psychologist E. M. Siipola reported in the *Psychological Monograph* this interesting study of set: Individual words were projected on a screen for a fleeting one-tenth of a second. The words projected were really not words, but **near-words** such as *chack, sael, wharl, pasrot, dack,* and *pengion.*

One group of people looked at the flashes of near-words with the expectation that they would be viewing words having to do with **animals** or **birds**. They expected this because those were the instructions read to them by the researcher. Another group expected to see words that were associated with **travel** or **transportation**.

Results. Siipola found that near-words were modified to fit the expectation of the viewer. For instance, the group of people who expected to see words having to do with **animals** or **birds**, reported *chack* as **chick** while the second group who expected **travel** or **transportation** words, saw *chack* as **check**.

Sael was **seal** for the first group and **sail** for the second group. *Wharl* was seen as **whale** or **wharf**; *pasrot* was modified into either **parrot** or **passport**; *dack* was distorted into **duck** or **deck**; and finally, *pengion* became either **penguin** or **pension**.

Set is extremely powerful in (a) filtering sensory signals to determine which will be converted into information (a process called *selective perception)* and (b) switching from one side of the brain to the other.

For example, Coralynn Smith, our head secretary in the Psychology Department at San Jose State University was despondent one day explaining that she had lost extremely valuable diamond rings that had been in her family for several generations.

When I inquired as to how the loss occurred, she said that in preparing her home for sale, she hid the rings because that Sunday, strangers would be roaming through the rooms in response to an "Open House" invitation. She hid the rings and could not remember where the hiding place was. I sympathized with her and advised, "Ask your right brain to locate the rings for you. It knows where you put them."

A week later, she announced jubilantly, " I found the rings. I found the rings." Here is what happened: The house was sold and after moving every piece of furniture out, she decided to take one last walk through the house which was now completely empty. She looked in every room and finally she looked into her bedroom clothes closet which was bare except for one lone hanger with a tissue that the dry cleaners use. She thought, "I don't need that hanger. I'll just leave it." But, on impulse she changed her mind when an incidental idea flashed into her head, "Well, maybe it will come in handy."

She picked up the hanger and there under the tissue was a string on which she had carefully attached the diamond rings. She recalled that as she was tieing the rings on the string, she thought, "Nobody will think of looking here for these rings." In this self-instruction, she created a "set" that nobody will think of looking here and of course, nobody included herself. The set created a classic case of self-induced amnesia.

The set told the left brain to instruct the right brain not to reveal the hiding place of the valuable rings. No matter how many times she asked herself, "Where did I hide those rings?" the right brain responded with an empty cognitive screen. The right brain had been instructed to keep the hiding place a secret so that nobody would find the rings, and it did.

The powerful impact of *set* on what we select to experience was demonstrated in this study published in the *Journal of Abnormal* and *Social Psychology* by Professor Solomon E. Asch of Swathmore College. Each student in a college class was given a written introduction to a guest speaker who was about to make a presentation to the group. The introduction that each student read was identical except for one word. Half of the class read that the speaker was "a rather **warm** person, industrious, practical, and determined." The other half of the class read that the guest lecturer was a "rather **cold** person, industrious, practical, and determined."

Results. Students with the word "warm" in the introduction participated more in the class discussion, and afterwards described the guest speaker as having more traits that fit a "warm" personality.

RIGHT BRAIN SET

The experiment by psychologist Siipola with *near-words* and the one by psychologist Solomon Asch with *written introductions,* demonstrated left brain set because the input to the people participating in the studies was verbal.

Either the right or left brain can initiate a *set.* If it comes from the left brain, then the content of the set is verbal; but if it originates in the right brain, the content is non-verbal. If the right brain provides the *set,* then there is no left brain awareness that a goal has been created. In Freudian terms, the goal is "unconscious."

For a classic example of an "unconscious" goal (coming from the right brain) and producing *selective perception*, consider this classic study with *anagrams* by research psychologists H. J. Rees and H. C. Israel. An anagram is a series of letters such as *lecam* which means nothing itself, but the letters can be rearranged to form one or more words. **Lecam** can be rearranged, for instance, to spell **camel**.

Here is the way the experiment works: People are presented with a list of anagrams and asked to rearrange the letters to form words. What the people do not know is that each anagram in the list can be reassembled to form a word using a code which is 34521 meaning that you start with the third letter, then the fourth, followed by the fifth and then the second and finally, the first letter. If you apply the 34521 code to **lecam**, the result is **camel** and **oryst** becomes **story**.

Once people have worked through the first list of anagrams *without knowing the existence of a code,* the researcher presents a second list that can be solved two different ways, either with or without the code. An example is **pache** which is **cheap** using the code or **peach** without the code.

Results. Most people solved the anagrams in the second list *using the code exclusively* — but strangely, they were quite unaware (at least, the left brain was unaware) that their problem solving was guided by a rule. We know that the left brain was unaware because after the experiment, each person was asked whether they used some rule or strategy for solving the anagrams and they said, no. Although the left brain was unaware, my hypothesis is that the right brain knew and was guiding the person's decision-making by using the code to solve each anagram in the second list.

My hypothesis is that the right brain creates goals for which the left brain is unaware. For evidence to support the hypothesis, consider the ingenious experiments in problem solving designed by Psychology Professor Norman Maier from the University of Michigan.

Imagine that you come into an empty room which has a string hanging from the ceiling at opposite sides of the room. Dr. Maier explains, "Your task is to tie the two ends of the string together."

"That's all I have to do? Tie the strings together?"

"Right."

Promptly, you take the end of one string and walk toward the other only to find that you cannot reach the other string.

Now what?

Dr. Maier tried many variations of the string problem to see how people would solve it. For example, in one experiment, when individuals from one group entered the room there were two strings hanging from the ceiling and in one corner of the room there was a table on which there was an unidentified metallic object.

Before individuals from a second group entered the room, Dr. Maier showed them the metallic object, identified it as a "telegraphic key" and explained how it worked. Notice that the left brain now has a **category** of "telegraphic key" for the metallic object and verbal information about the **function** of telegraphic keys. In addition, the people practiced sending messages with the telegraphic key.

Now the interesting question: Would more people in the first or the second group solve the string problem by using the metallic object as a weight that could be tied to one string and then start the string swinging like a pendulum? Once it is moving, walk quickly to the other string and return to catch the first string as it arcs toward you.

Results. More people in the first group solved the problem by using the metallic object as a weight. Why? The people in the first group had no prior concept (no category) for the object and hence, the object could be anything (even a weight attached to the end of a string.)

For people in the second group, the object was in the category of "telegraphic key" which includes the thought, "I know what this is and how it works." The left brain identified the object as a telegraphic key, but non-verbally (and hence, in the right brain) there is added, "and nothing else." By forming the concept, one draws boundaries which sharply demarcates what something is and what something is not.

Once the strange metallic object in Maier's string problem became a telegraphic key, it was difficult for most people to disrupt the concept and replace it with another concept. The initial concept had constancy. People who have a natural flair for problem solving are more skilled at replacing existing concepts with others. Probably this tendency to use **canvas** rather than **concrete** in building categories for data is what the famous developer of the automobile self-starter, Charles Kettering, meant when he said, "An inventor is someone who does not take his education seriously."

I do not believe that Kettering meant to imply that the inventor is an indifferent or apathetic student — only that the inventor is *sensitive to the tentative nature of information.* For example, at this moment, a concept may seem to be true, but tomorrow, it could be false, given new evidence. When the steam engine was first proposed for trains, scientists argued convincingly that the concept was unworkable because it was a scientific fact that human beings could not breathe at speeds of 30 miles per hour.

A remarkable example of using canvas rather than concrete for categories is the experience of Wilbur and Orville Wright who never received a diploma from high school. When the first gliders that they built in 1900 and

1901 did not have enough lifting power to get off the ground, the brothers concluded that all published tables of air pressure on curved surfaces must be wrong. (Most people who are successful in school would probably have concluded that the tables, because they were well documented and in print, must be accurate; and hence, it was impossible to fly.)

Since the published tables were "wrong," the brothers built a six-foot wind tunnel in their bicycle shop and began experiments to observe the impact of air pressure on the shape of wings. They tested more than two hundred wing designs in their tunnel. From the results of their tests, they developed the first reliable tables of air pressure on curved surfaces. These tables made it possible for them to design a machine that could fly.

WHAT IS REALITY

Concepts determine what we will "see" and what we will "unsee." Concepts determine what we will "hear" and "unhear." Also, each concept has an index of reality. This is the believability of the concept. It is the appearance of truth. The more people who agree that an idea is true, the higher the index of reality. For example, one of the greatest astronomers of ancient times was Ptolemy who published in about 150 A. D. thirteen volumes called *Mathematike Syntaxis* in which he pictured the earth as standing still while the moon, sun, and the planets circled at various rates of speed. The earth was, according to Ptolemy, the center of the universe in which the stars were brilliant splotches of light in a concave dome that arched over everything.

This concept of astronomic reality by Ptolemy was believable for 1400 years until the Polish astronomer,

Copernicus, offered an alternate concept in his master-piece entitled, *Concerning the Revolution of the Celestial Spheres,* which was published in 1543.

But Ptolemy's concept had a high index of reality. There was concept constancy which resisted disruption. It is understandable, then, that for 200 years the Church placed the works of Copernicus on the Index of prohibited books since it was "obviously" true that Ptolemy was accurate since one only had to look up and observe the planets to see that the sun, moon, and stars were moving around the earth.

SUMMARY

We see, hear, touch, and smell with concepts. Without concepts, we are blind, deaf, and unresponsive to input from touch* and olfaction.

Concepts are categories formed in the right brain, but can only be retrieved in long-term retention if the left brain accepts the concept. The existence of the concept in long-term memory depends upon the permission of the left brain.

Once a concept is admitted into the system, there is resistance to extinction from the left brain. There is

---

*A local television station in San Francisco presented a news story of a blind detective in Las Vegas who is able to differentiate cards by touch. How does he do it? He explained that in a deck of playing cards each card is slightly different in *weight* and *texture* so that by touch, for example, the Ace of Spades is instantly recognizable to him as different from the Queen of Diamonds.

From a day-after-day practice with handling playing cards, the detective has developed a rare "concept" (probably a non-verbal concept) for converting tactile stimuli into information.

"concept constancy." The left brain filtered what will and will not be retrieved from long-term memory. Once a concept passes through the critical filter of the left brain, the category has "concept constancy" meaning that the left brain will defend the concept from external threat (as from the introduction of a rival concept) and justify the category's continued existence.

Since problem solving means to alter or replace an existing concept, we can expect resistance from the ever-vigilant, ever-critical left brain. Unless ways are created to "quiet" the left brain, no problem solving can happen.

Problem solving (meaning that a concept is altered or replaced) can be achieved by "quieting" the left brain. One way to quiet the left brain is to adopt a "creative style" in learning which means that concepts are admitted into the system conditionally — with the caveat that a category is tentative until a better category (with fewer imperfections) is found or invented.

Another way to quiet the left brain is to create a goal to look for an alternate concept — a condition which creates a "set" for "selective perception" and fantasy generation until either a satisfactory alternative category appears or the goal is aborted. The tendency here is for most people to abort the goal prematurely when the left brain sends sabotaging messages such as:

It can't be done.

If it was possible, somebody would have thought of it by now.

It's impossible.

It's a good idea, but impractical.

I don't know what to do. Probably there is no answer.

If there was an answer, I would have thought of it by now.

There is evidence from the intriguing studies of memory by researcher B. Zeigarnik in 1927 at the University of Berlin that goals not achieved, continue to be active in memory. Children were given twenty simple tasks such as molding animals from clay, working a jigsaw puzzle, and naming twelve cities that begin with K. Some children completed all twenty tasks, while others were "accidentally" interrupted halfway through some of the tasks that were never completed.

The results: 80% of the children recalled more of the *uncompleted* tasks. The findings were confirmed twenty years later by researchers H. B. Lewis and M. Franklin and the phenomenon is known as the Zeigarnik effect.

A third way to quiet the left brain is concept disruption which means to destroy an existing concept — to move the concept from the green zone into the red zone as when an inventor presents an attractive rival concept for comparison with an existing concept.

In the next chapter, I will present many strategies that demonstrate how the left brain can be silenced so that alternative concepts can be found or created by the right brain.

REFERENCES

Asch, S. E. Forming impressions of personality. *Journal of Abnormal and Social Psychology,* 1946, *41,* 258-290.

Asher, J. J. *Learning Another Language Through Actions: The Complete Teacher's Guidebook.* (Expanded 3rd Edition, 1988) Sky Oaks Productions, Inc., P.O. Box 1102, Los Gatos, California 95031.

Asher, J. J. Toward a neo-field theory of problem solving. *Journal of General Psychology,* 1963, *68,* 3-8.

Lewis, H. B., and Franklin, M. An experimental study of the role of the ego in work. II. The significance of task-orientation in work. *Journal of Experimental Psychology,* 1944, *34,* 195-215.

Maier, N.R.F. Reasoning in humans. I. On direction. *Journal of Comparative Psychology,* 1930, *10,* 115-143.

Rees, H. J., and H. C. Israel. An investigation of the establishment and operation of mental sets. *Psychological Monographs,* 1935, *46,* #210.

Senden, M. V. Raum und Gestaltauffassung bei operierten Blindgeborenen vor und nach Operation. Barth, Leipzig, 1932.

Siipola, E. M. A study of some effects of preparatory set. *Psychological Monographs,* 1935, *46,* #210.

Zeigarnik B. Über das Behalten von erledigten und unerledigten Handlungen. *Psychologische Forschung,* 1927, 9, 1-85.

CHAPTER 8

HOW TO BRAINSWITCH TO GET A PROBLEM

FROM THE LEFT TO THE RIGHT BRAIN

Almost every book that has ever been written about problem solving is an attempt to transfer the problem from the left to the right hemisphere, and then create a "voice box" for the speechless right brain to "whisper" solutions to us. Later in this chapter, I will review problem solving strategies such as Brainstorming, Synectics and others to show how the transfer is accomplished.

A problem should be switched from the left to the right hemisphere because the left brain is not a problem solver. It can talk. It is logical. It can evaluate. It can think up a list of reasons why a "solution" will not work. It is rational. It likes to think in words and numbers. It is objective. It is "realistic."

But it is a deficient problem solver.

The right brain is the problem solver. If you ask it a question, it will find (or create) answers. If you present it with a problem, it will find (or create) solutions. Most of the "answers" and "solutions" will not be considered satisfactory by the critical left brain — but the right will continue to generate options — if you let it — until the left exclaims, "Aha, that's it!"

How does the right brain do this?

The right brain is not logical, nor is it realistic. It will find and create options with no editorial comment — no critical review. And that's OK, because being critical is the left brain's job.

The right brain is also literal. It will follow directions faithfully. This means that directions become extremely important. This is reminiscent of the ancient Arabic epigram, "Be careful of what you wish for because you may get your wish."*

Since the right brain is not critical, the "solutions" it produces can be constructive or destructive. The constructive solutions are, for example, inventions and innovations. Destructive solutions would be abnormal behavior in the classification of psychosis and neurosis including psychosomatic symptoms. Even mild aberrations such as defense mechanisms are products of the right brain.

In this chapter I would like to demonstrate how different problem solving strategies fit the split-brain model to produce constructive solutions.

BRAINSTORMING

The right brain shadows the left brain. Since the left is the executive, the first task is to send it on a vacation. Brainstorming experts call it "suspending judgment."

*As a poignant illustration, Claudette Asher Whiting told me this story. Her mother-in-law, Dolly Whiting, always wished for a modest amount of money. "Oh," she would sigh, "if I only had $10,000," and then she would create a scenario of how she would spend the money. This vignette continued for years and each time she expressed her yearning "not for a fortune, only a modest $10,000," she would have a different set of priorities for spending the money.

Then one day, a telegram arrived telling her that her son, who was a soldier in Korea, had been killed. As a consolation, the message ended with, ". . . you will, of course, be receiving his life insurance of $10,000."

When the left returns from the holiday, the right brain will have a stack of options in the cognitive in-basket. The left can then ponder the possibilities, cull out the rejects, and decide which option could best resolve the problem.

As long as the executive left brain is around, the right brain will be too intimidated to produce a stream of ideas — most of which are audacious and worthless. But somewhere in the dirt and debris sluicing through the miner's pan are glittering bits of precious metal.

As I mentioned in Chapter 2, when a person is under hypnosis, the left brain is "put to sleep" which permits direct access to the right brain. Hypnosis is a direct A to B brainswitch from the left to the right brain. Problem solving strategies attempt to produce a brainswitch while a person is in a waking state.

Osborn's concept of two minds. More than thirty years ago, an advertising executive named Alex Osborn coined the term, *brainstorming*. In his future-thinking books, Osborn pictured the brain as being composed of two minds: a **critical mind** and a **creative mind**. The critical mind, which we now call the left brain, judges, evaluates, criticizes, compares, and decides. This mind must be be neutralized if the fragile products of the creative mind are to appear.

The creative mind tries to produce novelty — new options, possibilities, solutions. It attempts to foresee, to predict, to anticipate what could be.

The critical mind (in the left hemisphere) is a power-ful executive with the authority of convention and reality as support, while the creative mind (in the right hemisphere) is a quiet employee who takes orders, works, and speaks only when asked a question. Even the answer from the creative mind tends to be hesitant, soft and lacking confidence.

This unequal power between the two minds — one is the employer and the other the employee — prompted Osborn to make this recommendation: Serious national problems should **not** be handled by legislators in committees. The reason is that legislators are expected, in the context of a committee, to be exercising sound judgment, to be logical, to be critical, and to make wise decisions. The critical mind is in full command of the committee meeting.

Osborn suggested as an alternative, that there should be two independent groups. One group which I will call "the idea generators" operate only with the creative mind of the right brain. Their mission is to suggest one idea after another to produce a Niagara of possibilities. Their task is **not** to (a) find facts, (b) find fault, or (c) make decisions. They are **idea generators** exclusively. The ideas are submitted to another group, the legislators, who then screen the ideas and select options.

In the academic field of higher education, I can say that in 25 years, I have never participated in a committee meeting in which the judgment-free, creative mind dominated. Always, one felt the over-powering presence of the critical mind. Always, the prizes went to reason, judgment, critical thinking, and realistic thinking. Participants were admonished for any behavior that was not reasonable, realistic, sound, workable, and practical. The meeting was closed to creative output.

I have speculated that highly educated people have a bias for the critical mind. Criticality is prized. Reason is prized. Judgment is prized. Correlated with this bias is a conservativism. Higher education, for example, in comparison with other organizations, experiences almost zero change in structure.

How brainstorming works. The first move in brainstorming (which is a classical brainswitching strategy) is to suspend "business as usual" for the critical mind. The critical mind is invited to take a holiday. Since the critical mind is reluctant to leave for a vacation, brainstormers are constantly reminded that, "no criticism is allowed" during a brainstorming session.

Next, the creative mind is directed to produce ideas, ideas, ideas. To keep ideas flooding down the cognitive sluice box since the gate is never shut with editorial comments from participants such as "that's silly . . . that's crazy . . . that won't work . . . or, let's get serious now."

The creative mind will continue to create possibilities most of which will be silly, crazy and unworkable, but scattered among the "fool's gold" will be genuine nuggets. Without an unimpeded flow of dirt and debris, there is little chance of discovering precious metal. Osborn calls this, "shooting wild." And the wilder and more bizarre the idea, the better because we can always engineer an idea to fit reality.

There are many tricks to increasing the flow of ideas. For example, Osborn suggested 75 questions to increase the volume of output from the creative mind because *quantity, quantity, quantity* enhances the probability that quality ideas will appear. Some of the questions are:

In what new ways could we use this as is?

How could this be modified to fit a new use?

What is like this?

How about changing the shape?

What color would be better?

What can I substitute?

Who else could do this better?

What to add?

Should it be larger? Smaller? Lighter? Heavier?

What can be omitted?

How can it be simplified?

How about reversing roles?

What can be combined?

In brainstorming, there is an **illusion of waste.** The high volume of unusable ideas are necessary for the appearance of on-target ideas. An analogy is the production of a motion picture. Hollywood producers anticipate that at least seven feet of film will be thrown away for every foot used in the final print. That's the minimum. The "waste" has been known to be a thousand feet of film for every foot that is finally used. But the "waste" was necessary to achieve the end product.

It is more economical to shoot a scene from many angles so that the film editor has options to select from in splicing together the final version. Without the options, most of which will be discarded on the cutting room floor, dramatic moments would be lost. Those details can make the difference in producing a box office success.

In brainstorming, another helpful concept is specificity in selecting the target of a brainstorming session. The more **specific the goal,** the more satisfactory the results. Also, Osborn advises that all ideas should be written down for distribution later to each participant. I believe that writing ideas on paper is important to establish the "reality" for concepts that are as fragile as the membrane of a soap bubble which can vanish merely from the heat of an approaching finger.

SYNECTICS

When a child asks, "What's that?" pointing to a strange, unfamiliar object and mother responds, "That's a tree" — we glimpse the process of learning. Learning is a *process of making* the *strange* into the *familiar.* Once the child has internalized the symbol and a concept, learning has taken place.

Once learning occurs, we shift from the **divergent** thinking of the right brain to the **convergent** thinking of the left brain. Learning is a brainswitch from the right to the left brain in which categories are created to encode raw data coming into our sense receptors. For example, before the child was told, "That is a tree" with follow-up information about the nature of trees, the child inspected the object and perhaps speculated about the peculiar details. Before a category is established, the right side of the brain suggested many possible associates (divergent thinking) in response to the strange object.

For the child, there is curiosity, speculation, and many rich associations — all of which ceased after learning was complete. After learning, there is no wonderment and puzzlement and searching for possibilities because one knows what it is. It is a tree.

From this point on, the right brain no longer transmits input to the child. Now when the object comes into view, the child does not inspect the object for uniqueness. The child does not wonder what it could be or what it could do. There is no speculation — no curiosity — no playing with associations.

The child *knows* that it is a tree.

To solve problems, according to J. J. Gordon, the creator of Synectics, we must start the right hemisphere working again as it worked **before** learning occurred. Our task is to **reverse learning.** Our task is to *make* the *familiar strange.*

How? By *inventing an analogy.* Gordon identified four kinds: personal, direct, symbolic, and fantasy.

Personal. In this brainswitch from the left to the right brain, you become like the thing you are attempting to modify. For instance, if you are trying to design a cleaner engine, you become an engine.

As you become the engine, you feel the up-and-down motion as the pistons rhythmically plunge down into their wells, then up to release gaseous materials. You feel the heat from warm oil bathing and lubricating your metallic joints. You smell the waste products being ejected. Just as actors in a play assume the role of another person, you assume the role of a machine.

As another unusual example of using personal analogy to solve a problem, a clinical psychologist told me about this case: The iron-handed black-and-white thinking of a parent was producing rebellious behavior in his child. The more the child resisted the authority of the parent, the more absolute and arbitrary became the parent's behavior. The more threatening the authority, the more the child resisted. The cycle accelerated at such a frightening rate that there was a risk that the child would be seriously battered.

The therapist realized that the parent's concept of authority was so inelastic that it could not be altered directly by suggestion. The other alternative was the child. The counselor told the youngster, "It's necessary for you to be the parent. You must be mature enough to modify your behavior so that — gradually, step-by-step, we can change the behavior of your parent. Tomorrow, here is what I would like you to do . . ."

When the left brain is presented with a strange configuration, it attempts to fit it into its existing geometry of concepts. It attempts to make the strange familiar, and if it can't accomplish this, it attempts to destroy the strange entity through rejection. An analogy is a skin or organ transplant. For a successful transplant, the donor's gift should be as similar to the recipient as possible because if the brain perceives that the tissue or organ is an "invader," it will be destroyed.

The left brain attempts to reduce the "scariness" of the unknown by making it familiar. People with a creative inclination are not spooked by strangeness. They find it a handsome opportunity. They attempt to make the strange even stranger to accelerate the output from the right hemisphere. One way to do this, as Gordon suggests, is to become the strange thing. While you are doing this, you dissolve the boundaries between yourself and the object and explore it in intimate detail with your hands, your feet, your tongue, and your nose.

Direct analogy. In this brainswitching strategy, we move from the left to the right brain by finding a *parallel experience.* Gordon recommends that we search for parallel experiences in unlikely places such as fields that are unfamiliar to us and distant from the problem we are attempting to solve.

He especially likes metaphors from the field of biology. Notice that the concept of "fields" sets up artificial boundaries that keep us captive in "our own field" where the territory is familiar. We feel uncomfortable crossing a boundary line into another person's field. But, that is exactly what Gordon recommends — crisscross the boundary lines into other fields in search of metaphors.

A classic example of crossing an artificial boundary line into another field is the work of Alexander Graham Bell. In a conversation with a friend, Bell confided that he was toying with a strange idea for sending sound along a wire, but he was about to abandon the notion because he didn't know anything about electrical engineering. It was not his field. Bell was a teacher of the deaf. The friend responded with, "You don't know anything about electrical engineering. *Then learn.*" Of course, that is exactly what Bell did.

I mentioned that Gordon prefers metaphors from

biology. In his book, Gordon tells how Sir March Isumbard Brunel was puzzled by the problem of how to build a tunnel underwater. The problem seemed unsolvable. One day, Sir Brunel happened to observe a shipworm tunneling into a timber. As the worm moved forward, it constructed a tunnel for itself. In a flash, Brunel realized that this was the analogy he was searching for which resulted in the classic concept of caissons.

In the previous chapter, I mentioned that once we set a specific goal for ourselves, the mechanism of selective perception is immediately activated to tune-in our cognitive channel to information that will help us achieve the goal. With a specific goal, when we look, we see, which is exactly what happened to Sir Brunel as he watched the shipworm tunneling into a timber.

The analogy that suggested the concept of a caisson would not have flashed into Brunel's mind as he watched the shipworm unless there was previous goal setting. Incidentally, usually the left brain (which is the executive) sets a goal that starts the right brain to work continuously and silently, on a 24 hour around-the-clock schedule, to achieve the goal using selective perception and fantasy generation.

I believe that people with a creative cognitive style instinctively use these brainswitching strategies in their search for alternative ways of doing things. For example, the famous experimental psychologist, B F. Skinner uses a curious strategy to find parallel experiences — that is, analogies that could solve a specific problem. He randomly selects a journal from thousands in his private library and then randomly selects an article to read.

Dr. Skinner's brainswitching strategy fits in with a nonlinear concept of how the right brain works. The right does not move, it seems, in a step-by-step logical progression. This may be, too, why UCLA professor Moshe Rubinstein in his book, Pa*tterns of Problem Solving,* recommends that in trying to solve a problem, a trick that often works is to open the dictionary *randomly* to any page and then *randomly* peruse the meanings of words on that page.

Symbolic analogy. In this brainswitching strategy, use poetic images to symbolize relationships. For example, a psychologist I know coaches cancer patients in the use of therapeutic images. One of the patients, for instance, symbolizes the cancer as a huge black rat inside of the person. When the patient experiences chemotherapy, he visualizes the rat swallowing the poison, becoming nauseous, and then becoming weaker and weaker and gradually diminishing in size.

In the *San Francisco Chronicle,* columnist B. M. Boyd published this analogy which moves us instantly from the left to the right brain for insight into the size of a molecule in an atom: A molecule in an atom is like a bumble bee inside a cathedral.

People with a creative style of thinking often perceive a problem with symbols other than words. This is an attempt to short-circuit the language-loving left brain. This is an attempt to brainswitch from left to right. That is, to shift from the left where words are literal to the right where words are used to create metaphors.

Non-fiction books that are best-sellers often translate technical relationships into metaphors. Apparently, even if one has no background in an academic specialty, a technical concept can be instantly understood if there is a brainswitch from the left to the right with an analogy. Most textbooks are "keepers of the secret"* — that is, by playing almost exclusively to the left brain, textbooks insure that concepts will be accessible to only a few people (those chosen few with "academic aptitude").

Textbooks do a brilliant job of hiding knowledge from most people. Textbooks usually have few, if any, analogies while non-fiction books are written with one analogy after another. Textbooks play to the left brain while non-fiction books play to the right brain.

For an example of a non-fiction book that is one analogy after another, see Eric Berne's *Games People Play*. In that book, sophisticated and complex adult behavior that is often incomprehensible when analyzed with the left brain, becomes instantly understandable with a brainswitch to the right brain using the analogy of games.

Freud used metaphors such as *ego, superego,* and *id* to explain mechanisms that drive human behavior. In the Harris' book, *I'm OK, Your OK,* Freudian concepts were expressed with even greater clarity using familiar parent-child relationships in the context of a family. For instance, at work, the boss is perceived as playing a parent role and the employee is the child. Each of us in relationships, function sometimes as a parent and sometimes as a child.

Fantasy analogy. Dr. Sigmund Freud hypothe-

*A term coined by my colleague, Gene Lynch.

sized that in day dreams and in night dreams, we generate one metaphor after another in an attempt to reach goals. Freud called it *wishfulfillment*. Especially in night dreams, analogies escape screening by the left brain as is apparent in the **illusion of reality** while we are experiencing the dream. That is, the dream may be illogical and bizarre when we review it after waking, but while the dream is unfolding, it seems perfectly logical, realistic and believable.

Hence, the metaphors created by the right brain to solve problems (that is, achieve goals) can be realistic or unrealistic, ordinary or bizarre, sane or insane, understandable or inscrutable, decodable or undecodable. One of the functions of a psychoanalyst is to guide the client in a decipherment of metaphors to discover what they represent in reality.

Gordon suggests that something similar to the therapeutic process in psychoanalysis will work in problem solving. One achieves this by pretending that logic does not exist. That is, one can short-circuit the left brain by the suspension of reality constraints which frees the flow of ideation from the right brain. For example, what is your wish if there were no limits, no restrictions, no impediments?

Sometimes an ideal solution becomes visible when all constraints are collapsed. Thomas Edison did this in inventing the electric light. While everyone else accepted the constraint that *light cannot appear in a vacuum,* Edison worked as if that assumption was not true and thereby achieved an elegant solution — the electric light.

OTHER BRAINSWITCHING STRATEGIES

RECOVER YOUR "LOST" PRIMARY LANGUAGE

Our primary "language of communication" comes from the right brain through body movement, drawing, storytelling, acting, gesturing, touching, pointing, and handling. For example, children in kindergarten are encouraged to express thoughts through the right hemisphere in activities such as *drawing, storytelling, acting, finger painting,* and *sculpting* with clay and other materials.

As children progress into higher grades, these modes of expression from the right brain are gradually extinguished to be replaced by communication almost exclusively by the secondary language of the left brain which is *reading, writing* and *arithmetic.* The message to students is that the symbols, designs, and pictures in paint, clay, and sand are "baby activities" reserved for those who are not yet ready for the important skills of communication — the 3 Rs.

Since the "under-used" skills of the right brain are gradually extinguished as the individual matures, Robert H. McKim in his book, *Experiences in Visual Thinking,* urges that we revive those skills since they provide a "voice box" for valuable and vital problem solving information from the right brain.

According to McKim, it is important for everyone to represent elements in a problem *visually* and *tactually* rather than always in words and numbers. Without visual and tactile symbolization, how else can we receive and transmit clear and audible messages from the right brain? Problems, McKim says, should be represented in *sketches, drawings, diagrams, patterns,* and *three-dimensional constructions.* Especially those of us who picture ourselves with zero art ability (incidentally, for McKim, the concept of "art aptitude" is a myth), should begin to rediscover those preschool skills that we once enjoyed. They may be more important in problem solving than the logical, linear syntax of words and numbers.

As further support, Stanford professor James L. Adams in his readable book, *Conceptual Blockbusting,* says that for high-powered problem solving, one must be fluent in many different symbol systems. Each of the senses has its own language.

As a hypothesis, all the senses operate from the right hemisphere using sights, sounds, smells, and touch as the elements of thought. Only when the sensations are encoded into words and the words are encoded into a line-by-line linear syntax are we in the left hemisphere.

Instead of being "multilingual" — that is, fluent in both the primary and secondary languages, most of us are literate in only one language which is verbal, and partly literate in the language of numbers. Our educational system is designed for fluency in only the secondary language of words, and for a few, the language of numbers. This is unfortunate because case histories of discoveries and inventions suggest that significant innovations were products of the primary language that operates from the right hemisphere.

Case histories. Across all the sciences and in business, one of the most powerful statistics for prediction is correlation. The concept of correlation comes from the genetic research of Sir Francis Galton who placed dots on a grid to show the relationship of height for sons compared with their fathers.

Visually, Galton could see on the paper that the pattern of dots moved in a diagonal from the lower left corner of the page to the upper right hand corner. Just by looking at the pattern, he intuitively realized that there was a significant genetic message because the sons of taller fathers tended to be shorter and the sons of shorter fathers tended to be taller. Height seemed to move from the extremes towards the center (that is, the average height).

Using the primary language of putting dots on paper to show a pattern, he was aware that one variable was changing in relation to another variable, but he wanted a mathematical way of expressing the relationship. Since he was not a mathematician, he approached a mathematical expert named Pearson who applied the secondary language of numbers to describe the diagonal pattern that Galton had discovered. The result is the universally applied statistical concept called the Pearson Product Moment Correlation.

The story of Sir Francis Galton suggests that mathematicians think in the secondary language of numbers. This may not be true as suggested by a survey sent in 1945 to eminent mathematicians all over America by Jacques Hadamard. These professional mathematicians reported that they did not think in sharp symbols such as numerical notation and words. Rather, they preferred visual and kinetic representations of problems. In other words, they used the primary language in problem solving even though the final, end-product was in the secondary language of mathematical notation.

One of the respondents in Hadamard's survey was Albert Einstein who said that logic, language, and numbers were absent in his problem solving. Rather, he would play in a vague way with images that were visual and muscular. Playing with images most of which were not logical or realistic — that is, playing with creatures of the imagination was more important than intelligence. "Conventional words or other signs have to be sought for laboriously only in a secondary stage . . ." when the playful images dancing in imagination have formed into a product that is comfortable in the world of logic. (Blakeslee, p.46)

The stereotype of Albert Einstein is that he derived his *Theory of Relativity* from complex mathematical equations that were scrawled line-by-line on hundreds of pages of paper. The fact is that Einstein as a young man was a clerk in the patent office in Switzerland. Physics was his hobby.

One day as he was riding home from work on the streetcar, he looked back to glimpse the time on the ornate clock located in the town square. Suddenly, in a flash, it occurred to him that if the streetcar was traveling at the speed of light, then at every point on the path from the clock in the town square to the streetcar stop near his home, it would be exactly the same time. The relationship between time and space is not absolute, but indeed relative.

Following this right brain experience in which Einstein received a message in the primary language of imagery — of analogy — he laboriously codified the thought in the secondary language of mathematics; and years later, experiments verified his hypothesis. For persuasiveness with academic colleagues, one cannot recount an experience on a streetcar. The revelation came from the primary language of the right brain, but communication with persuasiveness came from words and numbers, the secondary language of the left brain.

From the field of clinical psychology, there is a controversial example of brainswitching to solve serious problems of abnormal behavior. As I mentioned in a previous chapter, psychotherapy like education, traditionally has been directed to the left brain. For example, Freud, as a young physician, experimented with hypnosis to treat neurosis, but later used talking-out techniques such as free association and dream analysis. All three of Freud's approaches were intuitive attempts at understanding and remedying non-normal behavior through brainswitching.

Others to follow Freud, challenged his theories by offering therapeutic approaches that all shared a common feature which was **talking** to the patient and letting the patient talk. Instead of searching for analogies in the dreams of the patient and then trying to decode the right brain messages, the tendency was to **explore problems directly with talk.**

The patient talks about troubling issues and the therapist listens. Some therapists give advise and some therapists listen and ask questions that lead the person through a labyrinth of self-examination until the individual discovers a resolution. Except for psychoanalysis, most contemporary therapies use talking — the secondary language.

An intriguing exception is a therapeutic approach called the Z process developed by San Jose State psychology professor, Robert Zaslow. Dr. Zaslow hypothesized that "black" emotions such as hate and rage were producing aberrant behavior because people were unable to express these hideous feelings directly. Zaslow believes that a continuum of disorders from bed wetting to schizophrenia can be traced to the problem of coping with dark emotions.

It follows, then, that if the ominous, unresolved feelings can be flushed out of one's system, there would be a reduction in the emotional-electricity that short-circuits normal relationships. Talk, especially for serious behavior disruptions has not been shown to be highly effective. Talk seems to work in some instances, but no persuasive scientific case has been made for reliable and predictable results from any talk therapy.

Zaslow's Z therapy tries to produce in a person a peak experience of rage under certain controlled conditions. For example, the individual is cradled horizontally in the arms of the therapist and several assistants. Rage is induced by deliberately restraining the arms and legs of the person. (In infants, rage will be triggered by restraining the child's arms and legs.)

While the individual is restrained in the manner described, the therapist continually encourages the volume and intensity of hate and rage from the person. Since the entire body of the individual has the peak experience, this suggests that the right brain is the target of the therapy. I believe this is a right brain therapy that attempts to repair behavior through direct contact with the right brain.

The response to Zaslow's approach has been that many clinical psychologists and psychiatrists are horrified at the procedure. The repulsion may be resistance of people who are comfortable with left brain strategies. Talk is familiar and safe. To manipulate the individual's body to produce violent outcries, screams, curses, and struggling may seem to the left brain to be barbaric treatment. But, if it can be shown to produce reversals in abnormal behavior, then it deserves serious scientific consideration.

Rubinstein's strategy. UCLA professor Moshe Rubinstein in his book, *Patterns of Problem Solving* recommends a strategy which I think of as, *alternating brainswitching*. That is, switch back and forth continuously from the left to the right hemisphere. This alternating brainswitching is achieved by transforming a problem into many different models. For example, if you are expressing the problem in words, try numbers; if you are expressing it in numbers, try pictures; if you are expressing it in pictures, try a three-dimensional mockup.

According to Rubinstein, practice in how to transform problems into many different models may be **one of the most valuable skills** one can achieve in school. It is not enough to dispense information in one context such as in words or numbers and then ask students merely to retrieve the information. Short-term memory is not enough for effective problem solving. Skill in *alternating brainswitching* is critical for high-powered information handling.

Asher's golden gap strategy. A principle in psychology that has been verified in many, many experiments for both verbal and non-verbal learning is that *distributed practice* enhances learning more than *massed practice*. This means that if a person is practicing a golf swing, it is more efficient to hit a practice ball, then rest, hit another practice ball, rest, and so forth rather than hit one practice ball after another in succession.

The mystery is: Why should a period of rest (which can be filled with a different activity) between attempts at achieving a goal be beneficial? I call this period of non-movement in the direction of the goal, *the golden gap*. In the literature on problem solving, it is called *incubation*.

Even though we are not consciously and physically working to achieve a goal we have set for ourselves, the right brain, I hypothesize, continues to work for us. In fact, the right brain may need the "rest period" to search for information that will provide an answer to a question or a novel way of perceiving a problem — a way that transforms the problem into a non-problem. If we do not let the left brain abort the goal with thoughts such as, "It can't be done," the right brain will continue to work for us around-the-clock (even as we sleep) until the goal is achieved.

To demonstrate the power of the right brain in helping us achieve goals without effort on our part other than initiating the goal, try the human alarm clock experiment: When you go to bed tonight, tell yourself, "Tomorrow morning, I want to get up at . . ." and specify a time. At the time you have set yourself to wake up, you will wake up. Try it.

SUMMARY

A boundary line is an invention of the left hemisphere which has a yen for logic, order, and organization. There is safety if one draws a boundary line around one's territory and remains inside that familiar area.

A boundary is anti-creative. It produces convergent thinking. It produces restrictive thinking. It produces non-thinking.

"Knowledge" is gerrymandered into complex boundaries that are demarcated to warn where one can and cannot travel. The demarcations are called diplomas, degrees, licenses, specializations, and expertise. These boundaries arouse primal territorial instincts. One divides the world into "family" and "intruders."

Each concept (category) that the left brain permits to enter the individual's system has boundary lines. The boundary lines around a concept tell us what something is and is not. The left brain is organized to repel an invasion of a boundary or any attempt to modify a boundary line. Only with a brainswitch to the right hemisphere can we effectively erase boundary lines to allow alternate possibilities to be explored.

In the schools of the year 2000, perhaps we will recognize that one of the most powerful brainswitching skills for students is to *create analogies* and another is to continually practice converting "problems" from one language to another, (i.e., words to pictures, pictures to numbers, numbers to three-dimensional models).

REFERENCES

Adams, J. L. *Conceptual Blockbusting.* San Francisco Book Company, San Francisco, 1976.

Berne, E. *Games People Play.* Grove Press, New York, 1964.

Blakeslee, T. R. *The Right Brain.* Anchor Press/ Doubleday, New York, 1980.

Gordon, W. J. J. *Synectics*. Harper and Row, New York, 1961.

Hadamard, J. *The Psychology of Invention in the Mathematical Field*. Dover Publications, New York, 1945.

McKim, R. *Experiences in Visual Thinking*. Brooks/Cole Publications, Monterey, California, 1972.

Osborn, A. F. *Applied Imagination*. Charles Scribner's Sons, New York, 1957.

Rubinstein, M. F. *Patterns of Problem Solving*. Prentice Hall, Inc., New Jersey, 1975.

Wertheimer, M. *Productive Thinking*. Harper and Row, New York, 1959.

Zaslow, R. W., and Menta, M. *The Psychology of the Z-process: Attachment and Activation*. Spartan Bookstore Publication, San Jose State University, San Jose, California, 1975.

Chapter 9

Use brainswitching to learn the <u>second</u> most difficult subject in school

The famous mathematician, H. G. Hardey once said, "It is easy to be impressed by what you do not understand." For most people, anything mathematical is mysterious, impressive, and rather frightening.

After 25 years of instructing students in statistics, it seems to me that the first task in any mathematics course is to reduce student anxiety which is sometimes so exaggerated that students do not recognize their own name when it is called.

No domain of study has the exquisite beauty of mathematics because it is a territory filled with strange forms and shapes that fit together with a perfection that is nonexistent in the coarse world of things. The perfection of mathematical interrelationships, as Albert Einstein expressed it, gives one the feeling of looking into the secret workings of the Divine Mind.

One of the great mysteries is that the shapes and forms in the imaginary world of mathematics happens, in many cases, to coincide with relationships in the physical world. It may only be chance - a fortunate coincidence, because mathematical concepts are toys which were invented (some say they are the product of revelation) to delight and entertain those who enjoy creating with symbols much as a sculptor enjoys working with clay or marble.

Mathematics has the illusion of being reality-oriented and utilitarian when it actually is more of an art form. Mathematics is a deep-sea treasure hunt into an imaginary ocean of symbols to discover new patterns. Few of us, however, are delighted with mathematics in the abstract. The forms are too elusive for most of us. But they need not be.

I believe that the secret of understanding the "inner structure" (to use a term coined by the Gestalt psychologist, Max Wertheimer) of mathematical ideas is the **analogy**. Given the appropriate analogy, any mathematical idea can be instantly understood by most people. And, of course, when we invent an analogy, we have a brainswitch from the left to the right brain.

Another clue that understanding mathematics is a right brain function comes from the statistician, Richard J. Harris who said, "(I have) yet to meet anyone who could develop an understanding of any area of statistics without performing many analyses of actual sets of data — preferably data that were truly important to (the person)."

Since physical involvement is a channel to the right brain, Harris' comment suggests to me that mathematics like foreign languages is accessible to most people only when input is to the right hemisphere. When we apply a mathematical concept to solve a problem of keen interest to us personally, we are in touch with the right brain. According to Harris, this is the secret of understanding (via the right brain) rather than the usual left brain input of reading something in print or listening to someone talk.

Notice that the current mathematical curriculum is designed for a person (called the teacher) who talks and writes on the chalkboard while other persons (called students) listen and read. Hence, the input is primarily to the left brain. The result is that only a small proportion — perhaps less than 10% of students (those with high so-called "numerical aptitude") can learn the concepts. (Incidentally, "numerical aptitude" may simply mean that these individuals have the skill of receiving information on the left and then on their own, without the assistance of an instructor, brainswitch to transfer the input to the right brain for understanding.)

Most people can understand any mathematical concept if it is presented to the right hemisphere of the brain. I conclude that if we shift the design of our mathematical curriculum from the left to the right brain, mathematical instruction at all levels would be a smashing success.

BRAINSWITCHING EXAMPLES

I have discovered in my own mathematical instruction of students that *patterns* are often hidden by unfamiliar symbolization. Students understand, in one exposure, a mathematical concept if the pattern is visible, but often the orthography (printed symbols) used to represent an idea masks the pattern. For example:

In a mathematics class, during the derivation of a statistic called correlation, I will ask, "Who can solve this problem?"

$$N \Sigma X Y - N \Sigma X \Sigma \frac{Y}{N} - N \Sigma X \Sigma \frac{Y}{N} + N \Sigma X \Sigma \frac{Y}{N}$$

Few students will throw their arms in the air.

I then say to the students, "Let me try another question, which requires an honest answer. Who feels that they do not understand how to do this? In fact, if I were to press a Smith and Wesson to your head and threaten to pull the trigger, you would say, 'Go ahead and shoot because I can't solve the problem'."

Many hands go up. At random, I will select an individual and say, "Luke, you say that you don't understand. You can't solve this problem, right?"

"Right."

"What if I told you that you do understand? What if I told you that you can solve it? What if I told you that you knew the solution all along?"

"I wouldn't believe you."

"Luke, let me demonstrate that you do know how to solve this problem. The left side of your brain does not understand, but your right side does. Are you ready?"

"Go."

"Luke, I'm going to put some terms on the board and ask you to simplify them. Look at this: "

$$a \quad - \quad b \quad - \quad b \quad + \quad b$$

Luke smiles and says confidently, "a - b."

"Perfect," I exclaim. "Perfect, because that is the answer to the original problem. Luke, inspect the original problem again and see if you can detect the a, the -b, the -b, and the +b."

$$N \Sigma XY - N \Sigma X \Sigma \frac{Y}{N} - N \Sigma X \Sigma \frac{Y}{N} + N \Sigma X \Sigma \frac{Y}{N}$$

"Ahhh," shrieks Luke with genuine delight, "I see it! I see it!"

I have observed that students do understand a mathematical concept immediately in one exposure if the pattern hidden by the strange code is made visible. (**Pattern perception** is a function of the right brain.) Usually the code — the cumbersome symbolism — is generating noise. The symbols mask the underlying concept. And, after all, the symbols are arbitrary and unimportant. What is critical is the concept represented by the symbols.

For skeptical readers with a picture of themselves as word-persons who find numbers incomprehensible, try this:

Show that this term $\dfrac{\dfrac{\Sigma X^2}{N}}{\dfrac{\Sigma Y^2}{N}}$ is equal to this term $\dfrac{\Sigma X^2}{\Sigma Y^2}$

The right hemisphere of the brain knows the solution immediately, but the left may not. The left brain may be whispering, "You don't understand how to do that. Don't even try because you can't do it."

If you are one of the skeptical readers, let me prove to you that you understood how to do it all along. Let's take it step-by-step.

First, what is the name of this that I am writing on the board: 1/2

It is called a *fraction*.

Next, do you believe that if you multiply the top and the bottom of a fraction by any number, you will not change the value of the fraction?

Let's try it and see what happens.

The fraction is 1/2 and I will multiply the top and the bottom by 2. The top then becomes 1 times 2 = 2 and the bottom becomes 2 times 2 = 4.

The result is 2/4 which is equal to 1/2. So, the value of a fraction does not change when we multiply the top and the bottom by the same number. Let's try it one more time because it is important that the student truly believes* that a fraction does not change in value when the top and the bottom are multiplied by the same number.

The fraction is 1/2 and I will multiply the top and the bottom by 3. The top then becomes 1 times 3 = 3 and the bottom becomes 2 times 3 = 6.

The result is 3/6 which is equal to 1/2.

Now, back to the original problem:

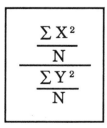

$$\frac{\dfrac{\Sigma X^2}{N}}{\dfrac{\Sigma Y^2}{N}}$$

*I have observed that at least three examples are necessary for students to nod in belief.

What name would you give to the display inside the rectangle?

How about fraction? It is a fraction because it has a top of $\dfrac{\sum X^2}{N}$ and a bottom of $\dfrac{\sum Y^2}{N}$.

I want to simplify the funny-looking fraction in the rectangle. My tactic will be to eliminate the bottom of the fraction.

To see the pattern (or the "inner structure"), let me replace the symbols with numbers.

$$\text{top} \quad \cfrac{\dfrac{1}{5}}{\dfrac{1}{4}} \quad \text{bottom}$$

Now I want to eliminate the bottom.

$$\cfrac{\dfrac{1}{5}}{\dfrac{1}{4}} \quad \bullet \quad \dfrac{4}{1} \quad = 1$$

But, since this is a **fraction**, I must multiply the top also by 4/1.

$$\dfrac{\dfrac{1}{5} \bullet \dfrac{4}{1}}{\dfrac{1}{4} \bullet \dfrac{4}{1}} = \dfrac{\dfrac{4}{5}}{1}$$

When you divide any term by 1, you get the term. For example, 5 divided by 1 equals 5. 100 divided by 1 equals 100. 4/5 divided by 1 equals 4/5.

Hence,

$$\dfrac{\dfrac{4}{5}}{1} = \dfrac{4}{5}$$

Now back to our original problem:

$$\dfrac{\dfrac{\Sigma X^2}{N}}{\dfrac{\Sigma Y^2}{N}} = \dfrac{\dfrac{N}{\Sigma Y^2}}{\dfrac{N}{\Sigma Y^2}} = \dfrac{\dfrac{\Sigma X^2}{\Sigma Y^2}}{1} = \dfrac{\Sigma X^2}{\Sigma Y^2}$$

Incidentally, what you have just done is the pattern (the "inner structure") that explains this mystery: In elementary school, we "learned" how to solve the following problem. Try it yourself.

$$\frac{1}{4} \div \frac{1}{5} =$$

Did you remember to **invert** the second term and **multiply** like this:

$$\frac{1}{4} \cdot \frac{5}{1} = \frac{5}{4}$$

If you were teaching this concept to children and one curious student interrupted you to ask, "Please tell me why you inverted the second term and multiplied." What would you say?

Most of us would not know what to say except that the rule is to invert the second term and multiply. There are two mysteries to be explained. The first is, why did you invert the second term? Why won't it work if you invert the first term? The second is, why did you multiply when this is a problem in division?

One answer that reveals the *hidden pattern* is this:

First, ask a student to tell you what these symbols say to do.

$$\frac{1}{4} \div \frac{1}{5} =$$

Maria raises her hand and explains, "It says to divide 1/4 by 1/5"

"Excellent. Now, someone tell me what this says to do."

$$\frac{\frac{1}{4}}{\frac{1}{5}}$$

Jeff offers, "It says the same thing. Divide the fraction of 1/4 by the fraction of 1/5."

"Bravo. Now, I will draw a rectangle around this ... and ask, 'What is the information inside the rectangle called?' I want a one-word answer."

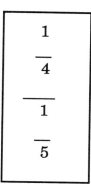

$$\frac{\dfrac{1}{4}}{\dfrac{1}{5}}$$

Dolores volunteers with, "It looks like a fraction."

"Good! It's a fraction, but it's a strange-looking fraction — a complicated-looking fraction. Let's simplify it."

The reader can see where this is going. First we establish that when you multiply the top and the bottom of a fraction by the same number, you do not change the value of the fraction. The students will only *believe* this after you have presented several examples. Then you eliminate the *bottom* with this tactic:

$$\frac{\dfrac{1}{4}}{\dfrac{1}{5}} \cdot \frac{5}{1} \quad = \quad \frac{5}{5} \quad = \quad 1$$

But, since this is a fraction, we must do exactly the same thing to the top. So,

$$\cfrac{\dfrac{1}{4} \cdot \dfrac{5}{1} = \dfrac{5}{4}}{\dfrac{1}{5} \cdot \dfrac{5}{1} = 1} = \dfrac{5}{4}$$

Notice that in the last step of the process we **inverted** the second term and **multiplied** it by the first term. The rule (which plays to the left brain) is a shortcut way of dividing fractions. But, the students now see where the rule came from. The *inner pattern is now visible.* The right brain understands how the division of fractions works so that it "makes sense" to the students.

MATHEMATICAL CONCEPTS IN MOTION

An interesting problem in understanding mathematical ideas is that many of the ideas are in motion. Unless the right side of the brain can visualize the motion, an idea will be fuzzy and incomprehensible.

In our usual left hemisphere mathematics curriculum, we present ideas that are in motion as if they were static. We use still pictures in textbooks or diagrams on a chalkboard to tell a mathematical story that should be told with motion pictures. Calculus is a classic example. Finding the derivative of a curved line is a concept in motion because as lines on the curve become shorter and shorter, the curve becomes a continuous series of straight lines and the slope of each line can be found with a linear solution.

In print, the explanation for calculus is fuzzy because it plays to the left brain. The concept to be understood needs a brainswitch so that the right brain can see the idea in motion. This can be achieved with animation on a video tape showing segments of the curve being transformed into straight lines as they become shorter and shorter. (I believe that "mathematically gifted" students are able, on their own, to make a brainswitch from the left to the right so that they see these concepts in motion. Everyone else is equally capable of grasping the concepts if the instructor makes the brainswitch from left to right with motion pictures.)

An analogy to mathematical concepts in motion is an attempt to explain in print how things function in the physical world. For example, what is the principle that makes a vacuum cleaner work? How about the telephone, radar, and air conditioning? Demystifying machines was the objective of a book called, "How Things Work." The problem is that unless a person already knew how a vacuum cleaner works, for instance, the explanation in print was meaningless. The reader needed a brainswitch which, I believe, is best accomplished with an animated demonstration on video tape.

Another classic example of a mathematical concept in motion is an idea in statistics called the Sampling Distribution. When I survey instructors of statistics and ask them to list the most difficult ideas for students to comprehend, the *sampling distribution* is usually at the top of the list. Even after several courses in statistics, graduate students still have a fuzzy, out-of-focus concept of the sampling distribution. The reason is that this idea is in motion, but we attempt to communicate it with still pictures in textbooks, print, talk, and diagrams on a chalkboard.

To demonstrate the problem of communication, let me express the concept of a sampling distribution in words (Please do not be disturbed if after reading the words, the concept is still inscrutable.): **A sampling distribution is a frequency polygon (or a histogram) created from a sample attribute, such as the sample mean, that was selected from every possible sample of a given sample size drawn from the population.**

The words in bold print above enter the left hemisphere and are uninterpretable unless the right brain can match the words with an experience of the phenomenon. Since the right brain is empty of a matching experience, the concept is meaningless to students.

In an attempt to provide a brainswitch for the students, I produced an experimental film several years ago called, "Sampling Distribution: Part I." To demonstrate the concept of a sampling distribution in motion, I worked with the late Allan Beyer for two years to produce an eleven and one-half minute film. The film production was time-consuming because each frame in the film is a still photograph. When the still pictures were spliced together, the result was animation in which students could see each sample being selected from the population, then they saw how an attribute such as the mean was extracted from each sample, and finally, they saw how the sample means were assembled into a histogram called, "The Sampling Distribution of Means."

As an epilog, the student reaction after seeing the film was this: "What a simple idea. Why did you invest two years of your time to communicate such an elementary concept?"

MATHEMATICS AS A RELIGION

Once students have the opportunity to brainswitch with mathematical concepts, students, for the first time in their lives, begin to think creatively about mathematics. Perhaps I should say that for the first time in their lives, they begin to think about mathematics.

As long as the information plays only to the left brain, mathematics is perceived as a religion in which one accepts ideas on faith alone. For example, when topics of a mathematical nature are presented, students suppress the tendency to ask "why" because "why-questions" are responded to with, "that's the rule" or "it can be shown that this is true" or "the derivation may be found elsewhere" or "it is obvious" or "that's a topic for the advanced course" or "simply believe me that this is true and let's move along."

Since "why-questions" are unanswered from elementary school through high school, there are two consequences. The first is short-term memory for mathematical ideas because the brain will not allocate permanent storage for false information.

Mathematical input is evaluated as false by the left brain because the validity of each idea has not been established. Even a "proof " in the mathematical sense is not perceived by the brain as evidence for validity — only as a meaningless academic trick that rarely makes sense. Remember that the left brain does not find novelty attractive (because it is unfamiliar and hence threatening) nor does it find falsehoods attractive. (As to falsehoods, I'm reminded of Mark Twain's comment that, "If you tell the truth, you don't have to have a good memory.") The left brain only wants to place truth in permanent, long-term storage.

The second consequence is that many non-sequiturs are not challenged by the left brain because it has been instructed by the authority of the teacher to be quiet. If the left brain had not been intimidated into a vow of silence, it most certainly would have responded vocally to this mathematical conundrum: When we were in elementary school, we "learned" that multiplication is repeated addition. For instance, two plus two equals four. That's addition. Two times two equals four. That's multiplication in which you simply added the number two twice. There seems to be a perfect fit between addition and multiplication.

Next, pretend that you are a junior high school teacher presenting a concept in algebra to junior high school students. You say to the class, "Someone raise your hand and tell me the answer to this problem," and on the chalkboard you write . . .

$$2 \quad + \quad 2 \quad =$$

The students smile and someone volunteers, "the answer is, four."

"Good, now try this."

$$2 \quad \bullet \quad 2 \quad =$$

Another student responds with, "Two *times* two is four."

"Excellent. Now how about the answer to this one?

$$(-2) \quad + \quad (-2) \quad =$$

"Easy," a student answers, "It's a negative four."

"Again, bravo. Now, one more time, try this..."

$$(-2) \quad \bullet \quad (-2) \quad =$$

And you say, "Remember, we are now multiplying. What is a minus two *multiplied* by a minus two?"

Since the children are logical, they have to reason this way:

We learned in elementary school that multiplication is repeated addition. For example, two **plus** two equals 4 and two **times** two also equals four.

Next, if we *add* a -2 plus a -2, the result equals a minus four. Therefore, if we *multiply* a -2, *times a* -2, it must equal a -4. All logic crys out for an answer of -4. A minus two **multiplied** by a minus two has to be a minus four. It has to be.

"No," you say when a student utters "minus four" as the solution. "The answer is a plus four."

"But why?" the students want to know.

"Because the algebraic rule is: In multiplying signed numbers, numbers with *like* signs will be positive and *unlike* signs will be negative. A -2 multiplied by a -2 are like signs; hence, the product will be a plus four."

Sound impressive, but the inner structure of the problem is still obscure to the students. What is the right brain input that will reveal the hidden pattern?

Let's brainswitch

For the past 25 years, I have presented this challenge to college students. " I want you to pretend that you are a junior high school teacher and you are about to explain to your students that a minus 2 *multiplied* by a minus 2 is equal to plus 4 and furthermore, there is no contradiction with that conclusion and the "fact" learned in elementary school that **multiplication is repeated addition.** Convince the children that multiplication is still repeated addition. Show them that everything fits together to make sense.

"I would suggest that you explain using a simple line like this:

left direction

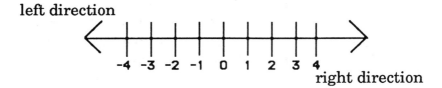

right direction

"Whatever explanation you invent, keep two thoughts in mind. The first is that when we do addition, a *positive number* means that you move in the right direction and a *negative number* means that you move in the left direction.

"Secondly, your explanation should be *symmetrical.* In other words, whatever rule holds for the positive numbers should also hold for the negative numbers since + and - only refer to a movement in the right or left direction."

Typically, a student will volunteer, come up to the chalkboard, and the conversation between myself and the student goes like this: "I appreciate your attempt at this, Shirou. Let's begin with 2 plus 2 and then move on to 2 times 2 and so forth."

Shirou picks up the chalk and says: "For 2 plus 2, you start at zero and move two intervals to the right and then two more intervals to the right. You end up at a plus four."

"Bravo! Now try 2 times 2."

"Well," says Shirou, "2 times 2 works the same way as addition. Start at zero and move to the right two intervals and then move to the right, two more intervals. We arrive at a plus four. Hence, you all can see that multiplication is nothing more than repeated addition.

"Next, let's try a -2 plus a -2. The principle for negative numbers is the same as positive numbers since plus only indicates a movement to the right and minus is movement to the left. So, start at zero and move two intervals to the left and then two more intervals to the left. The result in a -4."

I interject, "Excellent. So far, it makes perfect sense. Now, how about a -2 times a -2?"

"OK," says Shirou thoughtfully, "As usual, start at zero and move two intervals to the left. Since this is multiplication, you now *reverse direction* and move two intervals to the right and . . . Wait a minute," he exclaims, "we would wind up at zero. That can't be. Something is funny here."

"Shirou, not only do you get a -2 times a -2 as zero, but your model is asymmetrical."

"What do you mean?" he asks.

"Look, you moved two spaces to the left for -2, then for the next -2, **suddenly you reversed directions. Why?**

"When you multiplied negative numbers, why did you reverse directions when you moved to the left but there was no reversal when you moved to the right in working with +2 times +2? Somehow you must explain this strange imbalance to the children."

Other students volunteer, come to the chalkboard and attempt other explanations, but none seem to be satisfactory. With each false lead, the students become more excited and determined to resolve this seemingly simple-minded puzzle.*

Years later, former students will appear at my office door waving a piece of paper wildly and shrieking, "I've got it! I've got it!" And on the paper is the "solution" they developed.

The result is a fat folder with dozens of student "solutions." None are quite it. None have that "good fit" I have been searching for — but all show creative thinking (actually ingenious thinking) about this maddening number problem.

I would like to share with you the brilliance of the "solutions" invented by the students, who were, inciden-

*Attracted by the excited activity of the students, eavesdroppers at the open door of my classroom have often commented, "How can you spend time in a college class on a problem involving 2 times 2 = 4 ?"

My response is to remind the critic that Alfred North Whitehead and Bertrand Russell wrote a world-famous 300 page book called *Principia Mathematica* to explain that 1 + 1 = 2.

tally, non-mathematics majors. It is amazing how creative most people can be with mathematics when the context of instruction allows them to be in touch with the right side of the brain. Here are some examples:

Solution by R. Rinaldi. He explains the enigma of (-2) times (-2) = +4 with the analogy of a mirror. The first negative sign in multiplication is like viewing the number in a mirror, which reverses the image. Then when the mirror image is seen in another mirror, it is reversed again. Hence, the first -2 is a mirror image which is reversed by the second -2 to produce the original image of + 4.

While the mirror analogy is an ingenious interpretation of negative-number-multiplication, it does not account for the multiplication of positive numbers nor does the mirror analogy demonstrate that "multiplication is repeated addition."

Solution by K. Hom. She said, "Pretend that a positive sign means a **gain** and a negative sign means a **loss**. Then,

2 + 2 = 4 because a *gain* of two is added to a *gain* of two results in a *gain* of four.

2 times 2 = 4 because a *gain* of two is gained two times which results in a *gain* of four.

(-2) + (-2) = -4 because a *loss* of two is added to a *loss* of two which results in a *loss* of four.

(+2) times (-2) = -4 because a *gain* of two lost twice is a *loss* of four.

(-2) times (+2) = -4 because a *loss* of two *gained* twice

is a loss of four.

All the examples seem to fit together except for the last one. Something about it disturbs me. Does a loss of two gained twice result in a loss of four? It seems to me that the answer should be +2. For instance, if I had a loss of two dollars but gained it back twice, then I am two dollars ahead of where I was at the start.

Let's see how she would handle (-2) times a (-2). She would say that a *loss* of two is lost twice which means that we have *gained* four. This seems to work.

Solution by Doug Stocks. He said this: "Pretend that **plus** means that something *exists* and a **minus** means that it does *not exist*. There are only two states, *existence* or *non-existence*.

"Now, I believe I can show that multiplication is truly repeated addition. Let's start with 2 + 2. This means that you have two elements that exists and you have added two more elements that exist. The result is four elements that exist or, in other words, a +4.

"Next, (-2) + (-2) means that you have two non-existent elements to which you add two more non-existent elements. The result is four non-existent elements or a -4.

"(+2) times a (-2) means that you have two existent elements which do *not* exist twice. Hence, the result is a -4.

"(-2) times a (+2) means that you have two non-existent elements that exist twice. Hence, the result is -4.

"Now for the big climax. (-2) times a (-2) means that you have a non-existent two that does not exist twice. Logically, since there are only two states of being, existence or non-existence, it follows that if a non-existent two does not exist twice, it must exist. The result, then, is +4."

"Doug," I asked, "how would your model explain (-2) times a (-2) times a (-2)?"

"Easy," Doug answered. "You have a non-existent two that does not exist twice, so you have an existent four. Next, the existent four does not exist twice which means that you end up with a non-existent eight."

Each analogy created by the students from Rinaldi's *mirror image* to Hom's *gain-loss* to Stocks' *existence* and *non-existence* illustrates that anyone (even non-mathematics majors) can think creatively in the field of mathematics if they have the opportunity to brainswitch.

Interpretation by a professional mathematician. On an airplane going from San Jose, California to Washington, D.C., I debated for hours this "simple" mathematical puzzle with Dr. Richard Post who is a Ph.D. in mathematical statistics. Of course, the solution he offered is, he would insist, only an *interpretation*.

Dr. Post started by saying that he believed that **multiplication is repeated addition.** Here is how he explained it: First, when we add 2 + 2, we start at 2 rather than zero like this

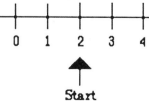

Now, add another 2 and another 2 to end up here:

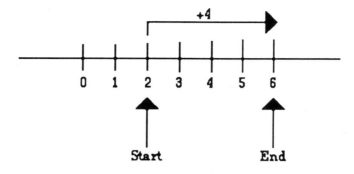

Figure 20

For 2 times 2, again start at 2 on the line and move to the 6. For example, you have $2 to start with. Now, you have $6. You are $4 ahead of where you were.

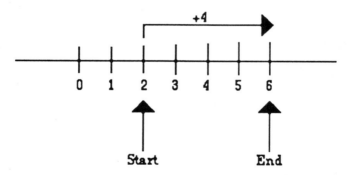

Figure 21

The debate became heated at this point because I was frankly baffled at the move from two on the line to six. I said, "All right, now how would you explain a -2 multiplied by a -2?"

He replied, "It works like this. You owe me $2. Now, not only don't you owe me $2 but I make you a gift of $2. In relation to where you were which was in debt for $2, you now have no debt and you have $2 in your pocket. Therefore, again in relation to where you were, you are $4 ahead. The answer is +4."

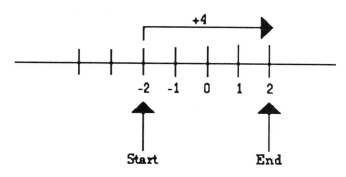

Figure 22

We continued to talk and never reached agreement on the reversal for the second sign in -2 multiplied by -2? Why, for instance, do we reverse direction when we move to the left on the number line in multiplication (when we did not **reverse direction** when working with negative numbers in addition)? Also, in working with positive numbers, there was no reversal in direction for addition nor for multiplication. Somehow, it seems to me, the elegant symmetry of mathematics is violated.

As I mentioned, for 25 years I have been searching for elegant solutions to the (-2) times (-2) = +4 enigma. I would like to share with you a recent insight that strikes me as a most pleasing resolution. It works like this:

SOLVING THE MYSTERY OF
MULTIPLYING NEGATIVE NUMBERS

In my book, *The Super School of the 21st Century*, I demonstrate how students of all ages can enjoy fast, stress-free learning on the right side of the brain *for any subject or skill* . While researching the chapter on mathematics, I discovered a fascinating book by Laurie Buxton, *Mathematics for Everyone*. It has scores of "motivational hooks"—mathematical mysteries that trigger the curiosity of students and start them on a strange voyage of discovery. I know because it happened to me!

From algebra courses I experienced in school, no one ever suggested that it was possible for me to create my own algebra and test it to find out if it works. In fact, I had the impression that there was only *one algebra* and only *one way* to solve problems. Algebra was algebra. You memorize the elements, operations, and rules—then start the wheels turning to produce solutions in a linear progression. *All very left brain.*

However, Buxton took the edict of *There Is Only One Algebra* and made it disappear when he mentioned the work of William Rowan Hamilton—who created *many* algebras (which was a novel idea to me). Even more intriguing, I discovered that Albert Einstein used one of Hamilton's algebras in the theory of relativity to predict the location of the planet Mercury.

Then Buxton convinced me that creating a new algebra is so easy that anyone can do it successfully. Here is how to do it: To create a new algebra, you list some element such as a, b, c..., list one or more operations such as addition, subtraction, multiplication or division, and state some rules. That's it! You have your own algebra. Your model is valid if it has no contradictions (as must be true of all mathematical models). If your algebra results in no contradictions, it wins a blue ribbon.

Asher's Algebra

Creating my own algebra was an irresistible idea that could resolve the mystery that tantalized my students.

$$2 + 2 = +4$$

and

$$(-2) + (-2) = -4$$

For *addition*, there is no controversy. Everyone agrees. Notice the exquisite symmetry. $2 + 2 = +4$ and $(-2) + (-2) = -4$. On the number line, to add positive numbers, stand on zero and walk right. To add negative numbers, stand on zero and walk left.

Now let's try *multiplication*. For simplicity, symmetry and logic,

If $(2)(2) = +4$ then

$(-2)(-2)$ must—absolutely *must* equal -4.

It cannot and should not equal a $+4$, especially if our elementary school teachers were correct in saying that multiplication is nothing more than "repeated addition."

How to Create a <u>New</u> Algebra
(In which $(2)(2) = +4$ and $(-2)(-2) = -4$)

Step 1: *List some elements*

In my algebra, I will use the same elements normally found in any standard algebra book which are a, b, c for constants and x, y, z for variables.

Step 2: *List some operations*

Again, I prefer to use the same operations in the standard algebra book which are addition, subtraction, multiplication, and division.

Step 3: State some rules

Before I reveal my new rule, let's explore what must be done to test the integrity of any algebraic rule.

The Critical Test for Internal Consistency

The test for internal consistency means that we will find no contradictions in the model. Let's see whether the Asher's Algebra has any contradictions when we apply the three properties of arithmetic: Commutative, Associative, and Distributive.

ASIDE: *When Jon, my typesetter, typed the words "Commutative, Associative, and Distributive," his eyes kind of glazed over... I asked him what he was thinking, and he said: "My left brain just kicked in with a few urgent messages. It told me that I don't understand this stuff (and never have); perhaps there's a missing link in my math education! Maybe I'll get it later on in the book — but then, maybe not."*

Arithmetic has certain obvious relationships that are made obscure with names such as *Associative, Commutative* and *Distributive.* The left brain scans these names and complains:

> "What is all this? These are supposed to be '*properties*' and '*laws*.' so they must be important — and they sound complicated! I wonder if I can understand any of it? What does it all mean?"

Let me take a crack at "simple" explanations. **Commutative** should be renamed *Number Reversal* because all it says is: If $2 + 3 = 5$, then reversing the numbers with $3 + 2$ should also equal 5. Multiplication works the same way. If $(2)(3) = 6$, then reversing the numbers $(3)(2)$ should also equal 6.

Associative should be renamed *Number Pairs*. A novel thought for me is the concept in arithmetic that we can only perform operations such as addition and multiplication *one pair at a time*. For instance, if we are adding a series of numbers such as 1, 2 and 3, we can add $1 + 2$ to get 3 and then add 3 to get 6. Another option is to select a different pair such as $1 + 3$ which is 4 and then add 2 to get 6. Try to predict the third option (the answer is noted below*). Notice that the explanation is more complicated than the concept (which is true with most mathematics).

Multiplication works the same as addition. You can only multiply *one pair at a time*. For example, $(1)(2)(3)$ can be multiplied $(1)(2)$ to get 2 and then multiplied by 3 to get 6. Another option is $(1)(3)$ to get 3 and then multiply by 2 to get 6. Try to predict the third option (the answer is noted below**).

The Associative Law (or *Number Pairs*) means that you can add or multiply the pairs in any order and get the identical answer.

Distributive should be renamed *Addition Dancing with Multiplication*. The pattern looks like this: $a(b + c) = ab + ac$. On the left, inside the parentheses, we are adding $b + c$ and multiplying the result by a. Whatever we get should give an identical answer when we multiply a times b and add the result to a times c.

---

*   Add $2 + 3$ to get 5, and then add 1 to get 6.
**   Multiply $(2)(3)$ to get 6, and then multiply by 1 for a final answer of 6.

We can have arithmetic without algebra, but we cannot have algebra without arithmetic. One test of a good model of algebra is: Does the model work with the three properties of arithmetic? We know that the sign rule in standard algebra seems to give strange results with the multiplication of negative numbers (i.e., $(-2)(-2) = +4$). Nevertheless, the sign rule does work with the three properties of arithmetic. That's why, after centuries of controversy and delay, the sign rule has become entrenched in standard algebra taught in thousands of classrooms worldwide. To refresh your recollection, the sign rule for multiplication is that like signs are positive and unlike signs are negative:
i.e., $(-2)(-2) = +4$ and $(-2)(-2)(-2) = -8$.

Here is a Better Rule!

But, is there a better rule? Is there a rule that will result in $2 + 2 = +4$ and $(-2)(-2) = -4$ and $(-2)(-2)(-2) = -8$, and simultaneously work with the three important properties of arithmetic? Yes, I believe there is:

> *When multiplying signed numbers (that is, negative numbers), use absolute values and multiply the end product by -1.*

First, let's apply the Commutative Law, which I mentioned should really be called *Number Reversal*—because all it means is that ab = ba. For example:

$$(1)\,(2) = (2)$$

and

$$(2)\,(1) = (2)$$

Let's see what happens with negative numbers using my novel rule that we *"multiply by absolute values and then multiply the end product by -1."*

$(-1) (-2)$ is transformed into $(1) (2) = +2$

Now multiply the end product, which is +2 by -1:

$(2) (-1) = -2$

Now let's try:

$(-2) (-1)$ is transformed into $(2) (1) = 2$

Now multiply the end product, which is +2 by -1:

$(2) (-1) = -2$

Voila!
There is no contradiction when the Commutative Law is applied.

The **Associative Law** states that when multiplying a series of numbers, any pair of numbers from anywhere in the series can be multiplied in any order without changing the final product. This sounds more complicated than it is. In algebraic code, it looks like this: $a(bc) = b(ac) = c(ab)$

Using positive integers, for instance, you can see that it doesn't matter what order we multiply +1, +2, and +3, the end product will always be $+6$...

$(1) (2 \cdot 3) = +6$
$(2) (1 \cdot 3) = +6$
$(3) (1 \cdot 2) = +6$

$2 \cdot 3$ means that
2 is multiplied by 3

Now let's try this with the negative integers -1, -2, and -3, using my novel rule. For symmetry with positive integers, when we multiply -1, -2, and -3 in any order, the end product will be —*absolutely will be* -6.

$(-1) \ (-2 \bullet -3)$ is transformed into

$(1) \ (2 \bullet 3) \quad = +6$

Finally, multiply the end product of +6 by -1 to get -6.

$(-2) \ (-1 \bullet -3)$ is transformed into

$(2) \ (1 \bullet 3) \quad = +6$

Finally, multiply the end product of +6 by -1 to get -6.
One more time:

$(-3) \ (-1 \bullet -2)$ is transformed into

$(3) \ (1 \bullet 2) \quad = +6$

Finally, multiply the end product of +6 by -1 to get -6.

There are no contradictions when the Associative Law is applied.

The **Distributive Law** can perhaps be understood on the right side of the brain with examples rather than a left brain verbal explanation which is more complicated than the concept itself.

In mathematical code, the Distributive Law is

$$a(b + c) = ab + ac$$

For example, with positive integers:

$$1(2 + 3) = 1(5) = +5$$

$$(1 \bullet 2) + (1 \bullet 3) =$$
$$(+2) \ + (+3) \quad = +5$$

Let's try it with negative integers:

$-1(-2 + -3)$ is transformed into

$$1(2 + 3) = 1(5) = +5$$

Now, multiply the end product of +5 by -1 to get -5.

$(-1)(-2) + (-1)(-3)$ is transformed into

$$(1)(2) + (1)(3) =$$
$$(2) + (3) = +5$$

Now, multiply the end product of +5 by -1 to get -5.

There is no contradiction using the Distributive Law.

Advantages to Asher's Algebra

Standard algebra presents the sign rule which is disturbing to children and adults who have encountered it in school. The sign rule is *"like signs in multiplication are positive and unlike signs are negative."* This results in the asymmetrical relationship of $(2)(2) = +4$ and $(-2)(-2) = +4$. Even though the sign rule passes all three tests for the validity of an arithmetic model (commutative, associative and distributive), it has been controversial for centuries among mathematicians—and only in recent history has it nudged its way into thousands of algebra textbooks.

My algebra also passes *all three tests* for the validity of an arithmetic model: commutative, associative, and distributive. The advantage is that my novel rule for multiplication of negative numbers results in the symmetrical relationship of $(2)(2) = +4$ and $(-2)(-2) = -4$. Not only that, but...

Negative Numbers now have Roots

There is a long history of mathematicians denying that negative numbers have roots. For example, what is the square root of -4? It can't be 2 because $(2)(2) = +4$. It can't be -2 since in standard algebra, the sign rule tells us that $(-2)(-2) = +4$.

With my novel rule, the square root of -4 is -2. How can this be? $(-2)(-2) = (2)(2) = 4$ and post-multiply by -1 to get -4.

Negative Numbers can now be Squared

If you square a number, you should be able to "unsquare" it and get the number you started with. For example, $(2)^2 = +4$, and we can "unsquare" +4 by taking it's square root. Thus, $\sqrt{4} = 2$. And 2 is the number we started with. *It works.*

However, in standard algebra, negative numbers <u>cannot</u> be squared because we cannot "unsquare" it to get the number we started with. For example, if you say that $(-2)^2 = +4$, then how do you "unsquare" this to get -2, the number we started with? $\sqrt{4} = 2$, but the answer we're looking for is -2. *It doesn't work.*

With my novel rule, we enjoy the symmetry of $(2)^2 = +4$ and $(-2)^2 = -4$. It is straightforward. Here is the application: $(-2)^2 = (2)(2) = 4$ and post-multiply by -1 to get -4.

An Added Bonus

Standard algebra invented the "imaginary i" for -1 in a valiant effort to make the sign rule work for finding the square root and squares of negative numbers. From this fairy tale creation came the family of "imaginary" complex numbers. The symbol *"i"*, along with its imaginary cousins, the complex numbers, disappear when my novel rule is substituted for the traditional sign rule. "Imaginary numbers" vanish into thin air from whence they came. My algebra has the enormous bonus of closing arithmetic for the set of positive and negative numbers within the domain of integers. This means that arithmetic with positive and negative integers gives results that are within the domain of integers without reaching outside for non-integers like "i" and "complex" numbers.

By applying Asher's Algebra, the square root of -4 = -2 because (-2)(-2) = (+2)(+2) = +4 times -1 = -4. Instead of inventing a nonexistent and intuitively disturbing "i" — my solution is an integer. This is obviously more elegant, if I do say so myself.

Note: for math buffs, my novel rule means that negative numbers also have primes for the first time in 24 centuries. For a step by step demonstration, see my new book: *Intimate Conversations with Great Mathematicians and Scientists—with never-before-published revelations.*

SUMMARY

Brainswitching has its greatest potential application in solving the second most difficult subject for students to understand in school, namely mathematics. The mathematics curriculum has been designed for left brain input (i.e., words and mathematical symbols) almost exclusively even though professional mathematicians themselves do not necessarily think and solve problems using the language of the left brain.

As Jacques Hadamard has shown in his survey of eminent mathematicians, including Albert Einstein, the preferred mode of thinking is visual and kinetic images which suggests a brainswitch from the left to the right brain.

Further, when students have the opportunity to brainswitch, most are not only successful in understanding mathematical concepts, but they can think creatively about mathematical ideas. Another benefit of brainswitching in the field of mathematical education is that concepts can be acquired without stress in one exposure - usually the first exposure, and as an additional bonus, there is long-term retention.

Solving the Mystery:
Multiplying with Negative Numbers

In school, we memorized on the *left side* of the brain, the sign rule for multiplying negative numbers: like signs result in a positive product and unlike signs a negative product. The sign rule produces an asymmetry that has baffled thoughtful students for centuries: If we apply the sign rule, not only is $(2)(2) = +4$, but $(-2)(-2)$ is also equal to $+4$. How can this be?

When my *right brain* is asked to explore this for a better answer, the result is beautiful symmetry with $(2)(2) = +4$ and $(-2)(-2) = -4$. This is a novel, never-before-published mathematical revelation that passes the three tests for the validity of an arithmetic model: commutative, associative, and distributive.

REFERENCES

Asher, James J. — *The Super School of the 21st Century.* 1999. Sky Oaks Productions, Inc. P.O. Box 1102, Los Gatos, CA 95031.

Asher, James J. — *Conversations with the World's Greatest Mathematicians and Scientists — and never-before-published revelations about mathematical mysteries.* (2001). Sky Oaks Productions, Inc. P.O. Box 1102, Los Gatos, CA 95031.

Beckmann, Petr. — *(a history of) pi.* 1971. St. Martin's Press, New York, NY.

Buxton, Laurie.—*Mathematics for Everyone*. 1985. Schocken Books, Inc. New York, NY. Distributed by Pantheon Books, a division of Random House, Inc., New York, NY.

Clawson, Calvin C.—*Mathematical Mysteries: The Beauty and Magic of Numbers*. 1996. Plenum Press, New York, NY.

Guillen, Michael.—*Bridges to Infinity: The Human Side of Mathematics*. 1983. Jeremy P. Tarcher, Inc., Los Angeles, CA.

Hadamard, J.—*The Psychology of Invention in the Mathematical Field*. 1945. Dover Publications, New York, NY.

Hersh, Reuben.—*What is Mathematics Really?* 1997. Oxford University Press, New York, NY.

Check out the following websites:

The Math Forum:	http://mathforum.com/
Ask Dr. Math:	http://mathforum.com/dr.math/
Problems of the Week:	http://mathforum.com/pow/
Mathematics Library:	http://mathforum.com/library/
Teacher2Teacher:	http://mathforum.com/t2t/
Discussion:	http://mathforum.com/discussions/
Join the Math Forum:	http://mathforum.com/join.forum.html

An archive of all the Math Forum newsletters and directions for subscribing can be found at:

http://mathforum.com/electronic.newsletter/

Chapter 10

Use brainswitching to learn
the <u>most</u> difficult subject in school

Mathematics is a high anxiety subject in school but most of us have some, at least basic, competency with many of the concepts. Foreign languages is a different story. Of all the students who begin the study of a second language in school, we can expect about 96% to "give up" before achieving even basic fluency.

Not only do most students abandon foreign language programs early on the learning curve, but they leave with the left brain storing the following destructive messages: "I can't learn Spanish (French or German). I guess I'm no good at foreign languages."

Only 4% of the population continues on in school with a long-term program to achieve fluency in a second language. Why? One explanation is aptitude* (which is potential, or capacity). This may be so, but the aptitude hypothesis does not explain why children with no schooling and with almost any level of intelligence, acquire a language with exquisite fluency — their first language.

Infants are fluent in speaking their first language before they enter school. Young children who move into a foreign country rapidly assimilate the alien language with a native-like pronunciation while their parents struggle for mere intelligibility. Can it be that children have a special gift for learning languages — a gift that disappears as they mature into adulthood?

*Aptitude to me is, "unearned skill."

I don't believe in either of those hypotheses. With the exception of pronunciation, the answer is not in aptitude nor in youth, but rather in which side of the brain one uses in acquiring the new language. The secret of acquiring another language — any language, at any age, is brainswitching.

The left brain myth

In school, at all levels, for all languages, the predominant instructional strategy is to design the curriculum for **left brain input.** For example, students are asked by the instructor to "Listen and repeat after me." Students are asked to memorize dialogues. Students are asked to memorize grammar rules. Students are asked to translate printed words. The intent is to teach children and adults to talk, to read, and to write directly. After all, the shortest distance between two points is a straight line; so, proceed from A to B directly. If the ultimate goal is for people to speak a foreign language, then let's get started immediately by having the student practice talking in the target language.

The problem is that human beings are not biologically wired-up to acquire a language, the first, the second or any additional language through the left brain. Nature's wiring diagram for language acquisition is visible when we observe how infants acquire their first language. It is through the **right brain.**

Before infants start to talk, they experience thousands of intimate caretaking transactions in which they hear directions in the target language and respond with a physical movement. For example, the newborn hears this:

"Look at Mommy. Look at Mommy." And the eyes of the infant move in the direction of the voice. When the child responds, the reward is excitement, followed by another direction from the father.

"Look at Daddy. Look at Daddy." And the infant's eyes shift to look at the face who made the utterance. **Looking** is the first physical response the infant makes to confirm that a message has been received. The infant may not understand the content of the message, but the response was appropriate. This is the initial communication between a native-speaker and an infant.

The "language-body" conversations between caretakers and the infant become more sophisticated as weeks go by. For example, the infant can now make an appropriate physical response to directions such as these:

"Give Daddy a hug!"

"Take Mommy's hand."

"Don't make a fist when I'm trying to put on your coat."

"Give your brother a kiss."

These directions to infants require a **physical response** from the child, not talk. The infant is asked to **look, hug, kiss, point, reach, hold, touch, stand, sit, walk** — all physical reactions that are input to the right brain. Parents do not demand that the child talk. Adults are thrilled that they can hold a conversation with the infant with spoken directions to which the child makes a physical response signaling that the message was comprehended.

READINESS TO TALK

The result of these "language-body" conversations is that the young child acquires a more and more sophisticated understanding of the strange noises coming from the mouths of people. Before any utterance resembling talk comes from the infant's mouth, the child has internalized a well-developed and intricate linguistic map of how the target language works and what the words mean. For example, an eighteen month old infant can respond perfectly to a complex direction such as, "David, pick up your red truck and put it in your room." In fact, the internalization of a linguistic map through "language-body" conversations **prepares** the infant to talk. Without the map, talk will not appear.

Incidentally, no one has ever directly taught an infant to talk or to walk. Talking and walking appear when the infant is ready, and **readiness to talk** will be triggered when the linguistic map has expanded to a size large enough to release talk. In fact, when the infant begins spontaneously to speak, you are witnessing the climax of language acquisition.

THE TALKING PHENOMENON

My hypothesis is that comprehension of the target language is the remarkable and graceful achievement of the right brain. It was not accomplished by demanding that the infant repeat utterances spoken by caretakers or memorizing grammatical rules. Not only do caretakers relax any expectations of talk from the infant, but when the child does finally babble an utterance that resembles a word in the target language, there is no correction of pronunciation. Instead of correcting the child's pronunciation to enhance intelligibility, the caretakers typically will mimic the distortions. Parents will use "baby-talk" that contains the vocabulary distortions invented by the infant.

In spite of this anti-learning behavior from parents (anti-learning because when parents mirror the infant's baby-talk, errors are modeled), eventually, the child's speech will shape itself in the direction of the native-speaker. Of course, as the child matures, the parents' tolerance for errors in pronunciation and grammar becomes narrower and narrower. What was a cute distortion at two, becomes intolerable to the parent when the child is five.

It is interesting that parents do not demand perfection in speech by insisting that the child repeat and repeat and repeat until an utterance is said correctly. For the infants, adults allow a wide tolerance for errors. It is amazing that the infant can self-correct when errors are rewarded with, "How cute! How adorable!"

To further "obstruct" the infant's speech development, parents will imitate the infant's bizarre vocabulary and grammar. (i.e, I overheard a parent say this to his child, "Does darling want an 'abdung' or a 'peepunch'?")

Brainswitching in the infant's speech development

The development of infant speech tells me that language is first understood in the right brain when adults say something, usually a command, and the child makes a physical response. In this process of "language-body" conversations, the infant begins to sort out patterns. The infant begins to decode the strange noises that are heard coming from people's mouths.

It is no accident that understanding spoken language comes first. Understanding may be tracing a linguistic map in the right brain which must be quite detailed before the infant is ready to talk. Notice, too, that talking cannot be forced or speeded-up. The child must be **ready** to talk before speech appears just as the infant must be ready to walk before toddling appears.

So, nature's plan seems to be this: Understanding must be achieved through the right brain before there is brainswitching to the left brain when the child is ready to begin speaking. Even when speech appears, comprehension will continue to expand and expand in the right brain. The comprehension map will expand geometrically and will always be far in advance of the child's skill in talking.

Brainswitching applied to second language learning

My hypothesis is that in acquiring a second language, we must first decode the strange noises through our right brain before the left brain is ready to talk. Then, the following instructional strategy (which I have called the **Total Physical Response**) would be logical:

Instructor: "Students, you are about to learn a new language in a very delightful way. When I say something in the new language, I will perform an action and you will do exactly what I do. Do not try to speak. Do not try to translate. Simply listen to what I say and do what I do. No work is necessary. Listen and trust your body to know what to do. Now I need two volunteers."

A volunteer sits on either side of the instructor. In front of them is a large open space. Other students in the class observe what is happening.

Instructor: "Levantense." (The instructor stands up and motions the students who are sitting on either side of her to stand.)

"**Sientense.**" (The instructor and the students sit down.) She continues a few more times with "Levantense" and "Sientense," then she says, "Anden" (And they all walk forward), "Parense" (and everyone stops), "Anden" (and they continue walking until they hear, "Parense.") Then the instructor utters, "De la vuelta" and they turn and are directed in Spanish to walk back to their chairs and sit down.

After acting out these motions with the students several times, the instructor sits down and invites individual students to perform alone in response to directions in Spanish.

The next series, with the instructor as the model, expands the complexity of directions with commands in Spanish such as:

"Point to the door."

"Point to the window."

"Point to the chair."

"Point to the door."

"Walk to the door."

"Point to the window."

"Walk to the window."

"Point to the chair."

"Walk to the chair."

Then, more expansion with,

"Point to the chair, walk to the chair, and touch the chair."

"Point to the window, walk to the window, and touch the window."

"Point to the door, walk to the door, and touch the door."

Notice that we are entering the right brain of the students with my instructional strategy called the **Total Physical Response or TPR**, for short. No talk is required. The student simply listens and acts quickly.

In this process of acquiring a new language through the right brain, you will observe a remarkable phenomenon. The instructor has inserted a set of strange utterances into the right brain. What if the instructor were to rearrange the utterances to create a sentence the right brain of the students had never heard before? Would the right brain understand a novel sentence — one produced by rearranging elements from familiar sentences?

For the linguist, Noam Chomsky, understanding novel sentences is the essence of fluency because if a human being can only understand the **exact sentences** one has heard, the development of human languages, as we know them, would be non-existent.

Understanding the novel sentence

To appreciate the significance of the novel sentence

in the achievement of fluency in a language, consider the pioneer experiment by W. N. Kellogg and L. A. Kellogg in 1931. From the Orange Park Anthropoid Station, the Kelloggs brought home a 7 1/2 month female chimpanzee named Gua. Her role in the family was to be the adopted sister of 9 1/2 month old Donald Kellogg.

For nine months, Gua was treated as a human child. She was diapered, bathed, powdered, seated in a high chair and fed with a spoon. She experienced the same intimate "language-body" conversations from her adoptive parents as did her "brother," Donald.

Gua did not babble, nor did she learn to utter any English words, but she did have an action language. For example, if she wanted orange juice, she would take "father" Kellogg's hand and place it on the orange juice bottle.

At the end of nine months, Gua understood about 70 utterances — only slightly fewer than Donald. There was, however, one dramatic difference between Gua and Donald in their understanding of English. Donald could understand when utterances were recombined to produce an unfamiliar sentence, — that is, a novel sentence that he had never heard before. The chimpanzee could not.

For example, the animal could give an appropriate response to these **familiar directions** that Gua had heard many times before:

"Kiss Donald" and "Give me your hand."

However, if elements in the **familiar sentences**

were recombined to create a **novel sentence** that Gua has never heard before such as, "Kiss your hand," the chimpanzee would be baffled. Her "brother" Donald could respond immediately to the novel sentence. (Incidentally, this fascinating experiment was replicated in 1951 by Dr. and Mrs. Keith J. Hayes who raised a chimpanzee baby, Viki, in their home. In spite of intensive efforts at language training by the Hayes', Viki never developed an effective use of language, but was able, haltingly, to say a few words.)

There is, however, a rival hypothesis to explain Gua's unresponsiveness to novelty in language that she heard. It is probable that Gua did not have the built-in biological circuitry for producing spoken language. But, Gua could express herself in a limited way by acting out what she wanted.

If Gua could respond by acting out what she wanted, this suggests that perhaps she could process information better in the right brain. If so, then what if Gua had been adopted into a family in which all the members were deaf-mutes? Would she be fluent in sign-language — that is, could she understand (and perhaps even produce) **novel sentences** expressed in sign language?

To find the answer, University of Nevada psychology professors, R. Allen and Beatrice Gardner brought an infant chimpanzee, whom they named Washoe into their fully-furnished house trailer to live for 2 1/2 years. During that time, the "parents" communicated with each other and with Washoe exclusively in sign-language.

At three years of age, Washoe had learned 160 signs and had even invented some of her own. For example, if

Dr. Gardner showed her a picture of a cat and asked in sign language, "What is this?" the chimpanzee replied by pulling at long, imaginary whiskers on both sides of her mouth. Another time, when one of the caretakers held a bib in front of her and asked in sign language, "What is this?" Washoe answered by creating this sign: She traced with her hands, the outline of a bib on her body.

It is interesting that most of the chimpanzee's communications were sentences with only two words such as, she would sign, "Open flower" to mean "Open the gate to the flower garden." Her signing lacked the richness achieved by deaf infants who demonstrate immediate understanding when familiar constituents are recombined to sign **thousands of novel sentences** the deaf child has never seen before. Not only can children who are deaf understand novelty, but as their understanding expands and expands, they begin "babbling" with their fingers to sign words. Comprehension of signs triggers "speech" through their fingers. And, once "finger speech" appears, there is a geometrical increase in the complexity of the children's vocabulary and grammar that the chimpanzee cannot attain.

Flashback to the classroom

As you recall, students acquiring Spanish with the Total Physical Response, could understand directions in Spanish modeled by the instructor such as, "Walk to the table" and "Sit on the chair." These were now familiar utterances that were firmly internalized through "language-body" conversations.

Students could give an appropriate physical response to familiar directions, but could they understand when constituents were recombined to produce a novel, unfamiliar direction such as, "Walk to the table and sit on the table"? Although students had never heard, the Spanish, sentence, "Sit on the table," they usually responded with perfect comprehension by sitting on the table.

Of course, the directions are short utterances to begin with such as, "Stand up," and "Walk," but within a few hours of TPR training, students are responding perfectly to novel, complex directions, as for example: "Dolores, when Henry draws a funny face of you on the chalkboard, run over to him and hit him on the arm with your purse."

RESEARCH FINDINGS

In the past 25 years, the TPR instructional strategy (which plays to the right brain) has been explored in many, many laboratory experiments (which I have conducted personally) and in hundreds of classrooms with children and adults learning languages such as English, French, German, Japanese, Russian, or Spanish (Asher, 1981). Since I have reviewed the remarkable results elsewhere in detail (Asher, 1988), I shall only summarize the findings here.

Learning in chunks

First, with my TPR approach (which simulates, at a speeded-up pace, the intimate "language-body" conversations that parents have with their infants), understanding of the target language is assimilated in chunks rather than word-by-word. By "chunks" I mean that students internalize the new language in large segments such as phrases and sentences rather than a laborious word-by-word learning.

Understanding novel sentences

Secondly, students demonstrate elasticity in being able to understand immediately any recombination of elements. **Comprehension of novel sentences** may be the most important skill in second language learning because it means that the learner can understand, as Chomsky expressed it, "an infinite number of sentences" in the target language. This skill in comprehending novelty is the essence of fluency.

Student output is greater than instructor input

Thirdly, there is maximum, positive transfer-of-learning. This is a critical feature in any language learning strategy (and in mathematics, too) because if students can only retrieve the exact input from instruction (that is, if **input equals output**), then the training has a low coefficient of effectiveness. For example, if students can only repeat the *exact content* of dialogues they have memorized without being able to recombine elements to express thoughts not in the dialogues, the student has almost zero fluency. In mathematics education, if students can only solve the *exact problems* presented in training, (that is, input equals output), then the students have almost zero fluency in mathematics.

As another illustration, if first grade students at the end of the school year, can only read the *exact passages* from books read in class, the reading program is almost zero in effectiveness. A high-powered reading program will enable students to enjoy positive transfer-of-training. This means that the *students are able to read sentences they have never seen before*. This is true fluency. This is skill in understanding novelty on the printed page; that is, understanding when familiar elements are recombined into unfamiliar sentences. Understanding novelty through transfer-of-training means that *output from the student is greater than input from the instructor.*

Transfer-of-learning across-skills

A fourth gain from right brain instruction such as the powerful TPR approach is that **across-skills** transfer-of-learning occurs. Amazingly, once children or adults keenly understand a substantial sample of the target language acquired through "language-body" conversations, they can immediately read when they see the new language in print. This is transfer-of-learning **across-skills** because what was acquired for one skill (i.e., comprehension), transferred to another skill which was reading. This represents an enormous saving in instructional time and is a dramatic confidence builder for the students.

Transfer to reading. Here is how transfer-of-learning across-skills works: Starting with "language-body" dialogues such as, "Stand up," "Sit down," and "Walk," the students internalize an expanding sample of the target language which becomes more and more intricate. After only about ten hours of TPR instruction, many students are ready to read. At this point, the instructor writes on the chalkboard in the target language or holds up flashcards on which are printed the limited directions in lesson one (i.e., stand up, sit down, walk, stop, turn) and then invites a student to participate with, "When I point to a word on the chalkboard, if you understand what it means, please do it." Most, if not all students, will respond perfectly when the instructor points to words on the chalkboard. (For an expanded discussion and examples of **across-skills** transfer-of-learning from one language skill to another, please see Garcia, 1988.)

We have discovered that there will be a graceful transition from comprehension to reading if the instructor is casual. That is, it is important not to announce to the students that they are "reading" because this alerts the critical left brain to intervene with sabotaging messages such as, "Oh, oh. This is different from what I have been doing. This will probably be difficult. I know that I won't be able to do this. I am going to have trouble with this because I don't know how to read Spanish (French, German). After all, we have had no instruction in how-to-read."

The wisest move on the part of the instructor is to omit the word, "reading" when making the transition **across-skills** from comprehension to reading. Notice that in the traditional textbook, the transition from one skill to another is signaled with boldface, enlarged print that is centered on the page and often is further highlighted by starting a new chapter in the book. This merely triggers the critical left brain which then sends messages that cause the students to be fearful and if possible, to escape from the threatening situation.

Transfer to speaking. The across-skills transfer-of-learning also works for a transition from comprehension to speaking. Once students have ten to twenty hours of TPR language training, most students will be ready to reverse roles with the instructor and utter directions in the target language to "cause" actions in the instructor and their fellow students. Again, we have a dramatic transfer-of-learning from the primary skill, of comprehension, to another skill, speaking.

Pronunciation. Of course, when speaking appears, like the infant acquiring its native language, pronunciation will not be perfect. There will be many distortions for most students. But gradually, as in the internalization of one's native language, pronunciation will shape itself in the direction of the native speaker.

Research shows rather conclusively that age is a critical factor in the achievement of a native-like pronunciation. If students start their second language learning **before puberty,** they have the greatest chance of acquiring a near-native pronunciation. **After puberty,** excellence in pronunciation is a rare occurrence even for immigrants who live for twenty years or more in a foreign country (Asher and Garcia, 1969, 1986; and Krashen, 1981).

For students who start the internalization of a foreign language **after puberty** (high school, college students and adults), a realistic expectation is that (a) with "language-body" conversations, they will rapidly internalize an understanding of the target language — in fact, in TPR classes, adults will internalize comprehension skills faster than children, but (b) children will enjoy an advantage in fidelity of pronunciation.

The pronunciation of the **after-puberty group** will be a normal bell-shaped curve in which about 10% will have excellent pronunciation in their first attempt at speaking, 10% will be at the other extreme on the curve and "mutilate" the spoken language while everyone else — the other 80% will be scattered between the two extremes.

Ramiro Garcia (author of *Instructor's Notebook: How To Apply TPR For Best Results*) has observed in 20 years of successfully using TPR to teach Spanish in his high school and adult night classes that the group in the middle — the 80% in the center of the after-puberty group will benefit most from coaching to shape pronunciation. The top 10% already can speak with a near-native accent and the bottom 10% do not seem to improve no matter how much coaching comes from the instructor. However, Garcia cautions that one can expect the students in the middle to show some improvement, but not a dramatic change to near-native pronunciation.

According to Garcia, the value of brainswitching (with TPR to the right brain) for children and adults means that everyone enjoys fast internalization of the semantics, phonology, and morphology of the target language. The high-speed comprehension of the target language without stress and with long-term retention is an exciting confidence-builder for students. In this extraordinary brainswitching experience, students now **believe** that they can learn a foreign language. They believe they can do it because in each hour of TPR instruction, they have evidence that it is happening to them and to their fellow students. It works for each of them personally.

With this self-confidence, students will volunteer to reverse roles and practice speaking in the target language starting with uttering simple directions which others hear and follow. With this self-confidence (which is rare in the usual left brainish approach that starts immediately with students speaking before they are ready), TPR students are willing to continue talking in the target language. And, they welcome suggestions from the instructor that will **improve pronunciation** rather than perceiving the instructor's comments as criticisms. Hence, students who experience brainswitching with TPR have more opportunity to improve the fidelity of pronunciation.

ENGLISH AS A SECOND LANGUAGE

Instructors in many big city schools, such as those in Los Angeles, find themselves in a classroom with immigrant children who have almost zero comprehension of English. Translation will not work to communicate since the native language of each child is often one of 26 different languages.

In this situation, the "language-body" conversations of TPR enable instructors to get in touch with the children — to start the process of communication instantly with zero stress for the children. Once the children are successfully internalizing without effort a **sample of English**, the right brain's linguistic map of the new language rapidly expands and expands hour-by-hour and day-by-day until the children are spontaneously **ready to talk.**

The brainswitching strategy of input to the right brain through "language-body" conversations worked also for the parents of the children. They enjoyed rapid comprehension of English, long-term retention and zero stress. But there was more.

The instructional strategy was to enter the right hemisphere of the adults by giving directions in English to move the students in a network of actions. After ten to twenty hours of TPR instruction, the students are responding rapidly and confidently to familiar and unfamiliar sentences spoken by the instructor. Now, what will happen when the instructor walks up to the chalkboard and **writes**,

"Stand up."

"Walk to the table."

"Touch the table."

"Point to the door."

"Throw your book to Maria."

"Make a funny face at Rita."

Adults who learned to read their **native language** of Spanish, French or German are familiar with the Romanized alphabet of English and therefore, can be expected to **read immediately** the directions that the instructor has written on the chalkboard. There will be an enormous transfer-of-learning across skills from comprehension to reading.

But how about the adults who are literate in languages that have a non-Romanized alphabet such as Greek, Russian, Chinese, Arabic, and Hebrew? Their printed symbols have nothing in common with English. How will they respond to the English orthography on the chalkboard that is unfamiliar to them? Will they enjoy transfer-of-learning, too?

What happens is that the instructor points to a direction on the chalkboard and individual students volunteer to perform the appropriate action. After some experience seeing the English directions in print and observing other students act them out, everyone, even those whose native language had a different orthography, can look at directions in English and execute an appropriate response. In other words, they can read English. Not only can they read familiar directions that they had experienced in "language-body" conversations, but they can also **read recombinations** — novel sentences that they had never heard nor seen before.

This is especially interesting to me since many people assume, from their memory of childhood experiences, that in learning to read, one must start with the basic elements of the alphabet such as A, B, C. The notion is that the student must master the letters, then words followed by phrases and finally sentences. This is a logical left-brain approach to reading. However, we have observed that if people already can read in their native language, we can skip to words, phrases, or sentences immediately even if — and this is astonishing — the printed letters of the first language are completely different from the target language.

SUMMARY

World-wide, foreign language instruction plays to the left brain in a direct attempt to teach people to talk, to read, and to write. World-wide, left brain instruction has not been successful with most students. It is slow-motion, high-stress learning with short-term retention.

As evidence, to cite only a few examples, the attrition rate of students in foreign language programs in the USA is about 96%. Elsewhere in the world, the picture is also stark. In Japan or Thailand, where English as a second language is included in the school curriculum for at least six years, the ordinary person such as clerks, taxi drivers, and waiters have achieved almost zero proficiency in comprehension, speaking, reading, and writing. In England, which is a ferryboat ride away from the European continent, the two year requirement for foreign language study in schools has been discontinued.

The evidence from 25 years of research (Asher, 1988; Garcia, 1988) demonstrates that with brainswitching from the left to the right brain, foreign language instruction can be fast-moving, low-stress learning with long-term retention. Insight into the biological circuitry for language acquisition can be seen in observations of how infants achieve an exquisite mastery of comprehension and speaking in their first language. This is accomplished without effort in what I call, "language-body" conversations.

In a "language-body" conversation, the adult utters a request such as, "Look at me" and the infant moves its eyes in the direction of the voice. **Looking** is the first physical response from the infant to confirm that a message has been received. The reward, of course, is elation from the adult and further messages are sent to the child such as, "Now look at Daddy. Look at Daddy" and the eyes shift to the face that made the noises.

As the infant matures and is able to make other physical movements, the messages become more and more sophisticated:

"Smile at me."

"Point to Grandpa."

"Give your brother a kiss."

"Give Daddy a hug."

"Pick up your teddy bear."

The adults speak and the child answers with a physical movement. All the while, the child is sorting out the patterns of the target language. The child is making sense of the noise. This comprehension map of language is being traced out in the right brain in finer and finer detail until talk is released. Talk appears spontaneously. It cannot be forced. It cannot be taught. It cannot be speeded-up. It will appear when the child is ready, and readiness to talk is triggered when the comprehension map has expanded to a sufficient size with sufficient detail.

I call this brainswitching, the **"Total Physical Response" or TPR.** We have discovered in study after study in the laboratory and in hundreds of foreign language classrooms around the world that most children and adults can acquire another language gracefully, rapidly, and joyfully when TPR is applied skillfully by instructors. TPR, in one summary sentence, means that we brainswitch from the left to the right brain by using "language-body" conversations that are so successful with infants acquiring their first language.

NEW DEVELOPMENTS

Since the first edition of this book, there have been some exciting breakthroughs in stress-free acquisition of another language. With my Total Physical Response as a foundation, there is an effective tool for making a smooth transition from understanding a target language at high velocity with TPR to speaking, reading and writing. That tool is TPR storytelling.

For children, I recommend the series of books entitled, *TPR Storytelling* especially for students in elementary and middle School by Todd McKay. For older students in high school and college, I recommend the *Look, I Can Talk* series for Level 1, 2, and 3 by Blaine Ray.

If you have worked with classic TPR, you know that the students have instant understanding of everything the instructor is saying in the target language. As a result, students of all ages experience remarkable self-confidence as revealed in comments such as: "I can do this! I was afraid that I would not understand, but I get it. I am actually enjoying this language class!"

Once students have internalized a batch of vocabulary and grammar in the target language with TPR, those items can be used to tell the students a very short story, then coach them to try telling the story to a classmate. Gestures are used to prompt the student step by step. As one young instructor told me recently on the telephone, "I was an average teacher, but these techniques of TPR followed by storytelling made me an outstanding instructor because my students are achieving fluency — not just ten percent of the class who will achieve no matter what the instructional strategy is — but 95 percent. It is extraordinary."

In the back of this book, you will find resources you may order to prepare yourself with these powerful instructional tools. For updates on TPR books, student kits, games and workshops, click on the web at **www.tpr-world.com** If you have questions, e-mail me at **tprworld@aol.com**

Free TPR Catalog upon request!

Sky Oaks Productions, Inc.
TPR World Headquarters Since 1973
P.O. Box 1102 • Los Gatos, CA 95031

Phone: (408) 395-7600
Fax: (408) 395-8440
e-mail: tprworld@aol.com
Web: www.tpr-world.com

REFERENCES

Asher, James J. The Total Physical Response (TPR): Theory and Practice. **The New York Academy of Science's** monograph, "Native Language and Foreign Language Acquisition," (H. Winitz, ed), Volume 379, 1981a.

Asher, James J. Fear of Foreign Languages. **Psychology Today**, August, 1981b.

Asher, James J. **Learning Another Language Through Actions,** Triple-Expanded Sixth Edition, Year 2000.
Sky Oaks Productions, Inc., P.O. Box 1102, Los Gatos, California, 95031.

Asher, James J. **The Super School of the 21st Century**. Demonstrates how students of all ages enjoy fast, stress-free learning on the right side of the brain for *any subject* or *skill*.
Sky Oaks Productions, Inc., P.O. Box 1102, Los Gatos, California, 95031.

Asher, James J. "Year 2000 Update for the Total Physical Response, known worldwide as TPR."
You can read this article on the web at: **www.tpr-world.com**

Cabello, Francisco. **Total Physical Response in the First Year.** (Can be ordered in English, Spanish, or French.) 2001, Sky Oaks Productions, Inc., P.O. Box 1102, Los Gatos, California, 95031.

Chomsky, N. **Syntactic Structures.** Moulton and Company, The Hague, Netherlands, 1957.

Garcia, Ramiro. **Instructor's Notebook: How to Apply TPR for Best Results.** 2001, Sky Oaks Productions, Inc., P.O. Box 1102, Los Gatos, California 95031.

Garcia, Ramiro. **TPR Bingo.** Year 2000,
Sky Oaks Productions, Inc., P.O. Box 1102, Los Gatos, California, 95031.

Hayes, C. *The Ape in our House.* Harper and Row, New York, 1951.

Kellogg, W.N., and Kellog, L.A. *The Ape and the Child: A study of Environmental Influence Upon Early Behavior.* McGraw-Hill, 1933.

Krashen, Stephen D. "TPR: Still a Very Good Idea." Novelty, Volume 5, Number 4. December 1998. You can also read this article on the web at: http://ipisun.jpte.hu/~joe/novelty/krashen_98_december.html

Márquez, Nancy. **Learning with Movements: Total Physical Response English for Children,** 1999. Sky Oaks Productions, Inc., P.O. Box 1102, Los Gatos, California, 95031.

Márquez, Nancy. **Apprendiendo con Movimientos: Método TPR Español,** 1999. Sky Oaks Productions, Inc., P.O. Box 1102, Los Gatos, California, 95031.

Márquez, Nancy. **L'Enseignement Par Le Mouvement,** 1999. Sky Oaks Productions, Inc., P.O. Box 1102, Los Gatos, California, 95031.

Ray, Blaine and Contee Seely. **Fluency Through TPR Storytelling.** Berkeley, CA. Command Performance Language Institute, 1997. (Also available from: Sky Oaks Productions, Inc., P.O. Box 1102, Los Gatos, California, 95031.)

Ray, Blaine. **Look, I Can Talk!** (level 1). **Look, I Can Talk *More*!** (level 2). **Look, I'm Still Talking!** (level 3). *Available in English, Spanish, French, or German.* Sky Oaks Productions, Inc., P.O. Box 1102, Los Gatos, California, 95031)

Schessler, Eric J. **English Grammar Through Actions.** How to TPR 50 gramatical features in English. Sky Oaks Productions, Inc., P.O. Box 1102, Los Gatos, California, 95031.

Schessler, Eric J. **Spanish Grammar Through Actions**. How to TPR 50 gramatical features in Spanish. Sky Oaks Productions, Inc., P.O. Box 1102, Los Gatos, California, 95031.

Schessler, Eric J. **French Grammar Through Actions**. How to TPR 50 gramatical features in French. Sky Oaks Productions, Inc., P.O. Box 1102, Los Gatos, California, 95031.

Seely, Contee **TPR Is More Than Commands At All Levels**. Sky Oaks Productions, Inc., P.O. Box 1102, Los Gatos, California, 95031.

Silvers, Stephen M. **Listen and Perform: TPR for Elementary and Middle School Children**. (You can order this book in English, Spanish or French.) Sky Oaks Productions, Inc., P.O. Box 1102, Los Gatos, California, 95031.

Silvers, Stephen M. **Listen and Perform: Teacher's Guidebook**. Sky Oaks Productions, Inc., P.O. Box 1102, Los Gatos, California, 95031.

Silvers, Stephen M. **The Command Book: How to TPR 2,000 Vocabulary Items in Any Language**. Sky Oaks Productions, Inc., P.O. Box 1102, Los Gatos, California, 95031.

Wolfe, David and G. Jones. 1982. "Integrating Total Physical Response strategy in a level 1 Spanish class." *Foreign Language Annals* 14:273-80.

Woodruff-Wieding, Margaret S. and Laura J. Ayala. **Favorite Games for FL-ESL Classes**. Sky Oaks Productions, Inc., P.O. Box 1102, Los Gatos, California, 95031.

FUTURE DIRECTIONS
for fast, stress-free learning
on the right side of the brain*

A paper prepared for European educators at the invitation of Alexei A. Leontiev, Secretary General of the International Association for Collaborative Contributions to Language Learning in Moscow, Russia.

Traditional left-brain approaches which we all have experienced in thousands of foreign language classes (including English as a Second Language) simply do not work. Perhaps a more charitable way to express it is to say that production-driven approaches which attempt directly to teach talking in a target language do not work well enough to continue the effort. The evidence: 96% of students who voluntarily enroll in foreign language classes "give up" after three years. Only 4% continue to achieve at least minimal levels of fluency. More damaging: Not only do our students "give up" but they are now convinced that they "cannot learn another language." After all, they tried but the results were high-voltage stress and the humiliating experience of failure.

What happened? The approaches seemed to be sound and rooted in common sense. For example, we know from our high school geometry that the shortest distance between two points is a straight line. So, let's proceed from A to B directly in a straight line. If you want to acquire another language, then "listen and repeat after me!" "Memorize this dialogue" and "Let me explain the grammar rule for the day." What could be more transparent as an instructional strategy?

But it did not work. The laboratory research and practical experience in thousands of foreign language classrooms indicated

---

*This article is also available by clicking on: **www.tpr—world.com***

that one human being cannot directly teach another human being to talk. Apparently we are not biologically wired up to acquire a language in that fashion. Leslie A. Hart would say that the traditional approach of "teaching" children and adults to speak another language is simply brain antagonistic. The approach does not fit our knowledge of how the brain functions.

It sounds like pedagogical heresy. Of course one person can directly teach another person to talk. It seems obvious, but this belief turns out to be an illusion, a myth that has persisted generation after generation with the fallout being a massive experience of failure not only for students but also for instructors. If teaching students to talk was successful then we would not have this situation in the USA: Of the 500,000 young Americans stationed in the military throughout the world, only 418 were judged to be linguistically competent to communicate in the language of the host country. Japan and other Asian countries, where learning English is a national craze, schools carry children through six years of English as a foreign language. Still, only a few students break the fluency barrier to achieve communication skills in English.

Recently, on a trip to Europe we met a colleague, Dr. Francisco Cabello, who has lived most of his life in Seville, Spain and is a Professor of Spanish at famous Concordia College's Language Villages in Minnesota. He authored the successful series of books "The Total Physical Response in First Year English, Spanish and French." I asked him, "How successful do you think second language learning is in Spain?"

Dr. Cabello: "Not very. Parents are frenetic to find a way for their children to acquire English. They spend a fortune on private lessons after school. You see full page ads in the paper and expensive television commercials for private language courses, especially for learning English. This is probably true in the surrounding countries, as well."

Asher: "And the result?"

Dr. Cabello: "Well, you don't hear people speaking English anywhere do you?"

Asher: "How do you explain this?'

Dr. Cabello: "They use traditional instructional strategies such as grammar-translation and listen and repeat after me.

Asher: "All brain antagonistic approaches, especially in the initial and even intermediate stages of language learning."

Dr. Cabello: "Yes. These programs try to ram the skill into the student through the left brain. It doesn't work but they don't know what else to do. A few students can tolerate the stress and eventually acquire enough skill to function in the target language but most do not."

Asher: "Why do you think that grammar-translation has held on so long ?

Dr. Cabello: "I think it is more comfortable for instructors who are not native speakers of the target language. They are off the hook. When they speak in the target language, they are anxious that their pronunciation may not be perfect. So, to escape any criticism, the safe approach is to ask the students to take out pencil and paper and start translating. I don't think it is more complicated than that."

A Brain Compatible Instructional Strategy

...that works for most students who are acquiring second languages, mathematics, and science.

Historically, school has played to the left side of the brain almost exclusively from the third grade through the university. In classrooms, the arrangement of chairs is in a pattern that is comfortable for left brain instruction. Students sitting in rows and columns face one direction to receive information that will be delivered in serial order through verbal media either in speech or in print. Input is to half of the brain—the left side. Students who are "academically gifted" can, on their own, switch the information coming into the left brain over to the right brain for complete processing to achieve meaning.

A classic example is a study by Jacques Hadamard of how eminent mathematicians think. The stereotype is that these professionals think in sharp symbols and equations—in other words, they are processing information exclusively on the left side of the brain. But Hadamard discovered that outstanding mathematicians think in visual and kinetic images. One of the people in the study was Einstein who confided that he visualized events in motion and he added that he felt that imagination was more important in mathematics and physics than intelligence. Of course, visualization and motion is processing information through the right brain. But school is organized, unintentionally to be sure, to shut down the right brain.

For example, notice that as instructors we give ourselves the advantage of using the right brain when we move about the classroom in our delivery of information. Movement of our body makes information flow from left to right and back again at lightning velocity. But we do not accord our students the same privilege. They must sit and "pay attention" to us as we move about the scene. We allow only limited movement from students as when they move their arms to scribble a note or raise their hands occasionally to ask a question. If you think back on all the classes you have attended, can you recall any instructor in any grade from the first through the university who sat with hands folded for 75 minutes and talked?

With the realization that the student's body and the student's body movements are my best allies in helping students internalize information, I always encourage my students in statistics courses to move about the room frequently. "If it helps" I tell them, "please feel free to get up anytime and walk out for a drink of water or to go to the restroom or simply walk around the back of the room or move from one side of the room to the other for a different perspective of the scene." Also, I reverse roles continually to permit students the movement privilege bestowed upon teachers. For instance, at the start of each class meeting, I will invite students to present their work on the board so that everyone is continually moving to the chalkboard to reverse roles with me. Incidentally, I usually invite students to present their work in pairs rather than alone. This strategy neutralizes the fear generated by the critical left brain that, "Oh, no. You have to go up to the front of the room and speak in public!" Remember that the worst fear people have is speaking in public.

The Power of Movement
in Acquiring Another Language

By now most language teachers in the United States and Canada have heard about my Total Physical Response (TPR) approach. In 25 years of laboratory research and thousands of classrooms, we have demonstrated that TPR can be applied as the major focus of language instruction or as an effective supplement. However, few language instructors outside North America are aware of the dramatic differences that can be achieved in their instructional program with TPR.

The benefits of TPR are (a) rapid understanding of the target language, (b) long-term retention lasting weeks, months, even years, and (c) zero stress for both students and the instructor. The principle of TPR is deceptively simple—it is simple to understand, but does require skillful application to be effective.

The principle of TPR may be seen in the interaction of adults and infants in intimate caretaking transactions. If you observe carefully, you will witness in the caretaking experience a continual conversation between adults and the infant. It is, of course, not the usual conversation in which talk is uttered back and forth between two or more people. It is a unique conversation in which the adult talks to the infant and the infant answers with a physical response that is meaningful to the adult. For example, the baby can be only days old and an adult will say, "Look at me. Look at me." The baby turns its head in the direction of the voice and the adult exclaims with delight, "She is looking at me!" Another person says, "Now look at Daddy! Look at Daddy!" The infant turns in the direction of the voice and smiles. I call these unique conversations in caretaking, "language-body conversations." The adult speaks and the infant answers with a physical response such as turning the head, smiling, crying, reaching, grasping, walking, etc. Caretaking is a rich networking of language-body conversations that continues 16 hours a day for years.

During the period of birth to about two years of age, there will be continual language-body conversations between caretakers and the neonate, but the infant's talk will be limited to a few single utterances that are distortions of such words as mother, father, water, go, swing, drink, bottle, etc. However, the stunning feature of a language-body conversation is that before even "mommy" or "daddy" becomes clearly articulated, the infant demonstrates perfect understanding by physically responding to complex directions from the adult such as, "Pick up your toys from the sofa, and put them on the bed in your room." The infant demonstrates perfect understanding of complex sentences even though the baby is barely able to utter a single word.

The first achievement in language acquisition is exquisite skill in understanding the target language. I call this understanding *comprehension literacy.* Observations of infants show that most babies internalize, through body movements, an intricate linguistic map of how the language works *before the infant is ready to talk.* And when talk appears, it will be fragmented, distorted, and primitive compared with a fluent understanding of the target language. Furthermore, throughout the child's development, production will lag far behind comprehension. Language acquisition is clearly a linear progression with comprehension first, then production. Never do we observe infants in any culture or in any historical period showing language acquisition starting with production followed by comprehension.

The phenomenon of comprehension followed by production is so striking that it suggests a design in the brain and nervous system with "biological wiring" programmed like this: Talk will not be triggered until the infant has internalized enough details in the linguistic map. Clearly, the triggering mechanism for production is *comprehension literacy.* Biological wiring is not a metaphor, but has definite reference points in the brain as suggested by Broca's Area (located in the frontal region of the left hemisphere) which, if damaged, disturbs speech and Wernicke's Area (located in the posterior region of the first temporal gyrus) which, if injured, produces impaired comprehension of speech.

It is significant that the location in the brain for speech and comprehension is distinctly different. For example, the clinical literature has many case histories of brain injured patients who can speak but cannot comprehend sentences uttered by others, and other patients who can comprehend what is said to them but cannot speak. Future research with high-technology brain scanning equipment will probably show that the infant's brain first lights the circuitry in Wernicke's Area with intense neuro-electrical activity that continues for many months before the circuitry in Broca's Area becomes busy.

Incidentally, there is no evidence that the "biological wiring" for language acquisition changes as the infant develops into childhood and then adulthood. And, indeed, our experiments (Asher, 2000) together with classroom observations of children and adults (Garcia, 2001) suggest that a linear progression from comprehension to production is imperative for most students (perhaps 95%) if they are to achieve multi-skill fluency in a second language. The evidence is clear, however, that a "progression" starting with production (teaching children and adults to talk, read or write) is an illusion since it results in a success rate of only 4% (Asher, 2000).

Comprehension Literacy
How to help second language learners achieve it

If comprehension is a critical first step in the language acquisition process to give students a "head start," then how to proceed? Fortunately, several dozen books together with video demonstrations are now available to guide language instructors step-by-step. I have listed many of them in the references at the end of this article. If you choose to apply the Total Physical Response to help your students achieve comprehension literacy, then I recommend that you start with my book, *Learning Another Language Through Actions* which explains the theory, summarizes the research, answers the most often-asked-questions about TPR, and then presents practical day-to-day lessons for 150 hours of classroom instruction.

For additional practical lessons and hundreds of valuable tips for a successful TPR experience with your students, I recommend Ramiro Garcia's book, *Instructor's Notebook: How To Apply TPR For Best Results.* In the second edition of my book, *Brainswitching: Learning on the Right Side of the Brain*, you will find hundreds of practical examples that demonstrate how to use movement (and other high-powered techniques to transfer information from the left to the right brain. This switching from one side of the brain to the other helps students achieve stress-free internalization of "complex" concepts in mathematics and science. For more suggestions on how to implement successful right brain teaching, see my book: **The Super School of the 21st Century**.

Classroom Applications

Infants acquire language during *language-body conversations* with their parents. When students in the classroom have *language-body conversations* with their instructor, they achieve comprehension significantly faster than infants. Here is the reason: infants are limited in their range of physical responses. School children and adults, by comparison, enjoy a vast network of physical movements such as writing, cooking, drawing pictures, driving vehicles, playing games, operating computers, riding bicycles, and so on. Fluent understanding that takes years for infants to acquire can be achieved by students in a fraction of the time using TPR.

Here is a sample of a language-body conversation in the classroom: We begin with what Dr. David Wolfe, a master TPR instructor of French and Spanish working in the Philadelphia schools, calls the "big eight"—that is single commands of stand, sit, walk, turn, run, stop, squat, and jump.

Typically, the instructor will invite a student to sit on either side and listen carefully to what the instructor will utter in the target language (with no translation) and do exactly what they see the instructor doing. (To further relax students, they are briefed that they are to be silent and not attempt to pronounce any of the utterances they will be hearing.) The instructions are, "Relax, be comfortable, listen, watch what I do and do exactly the same thing. I will not ask you to pronounce any of the utterances you will be hearing."

The instructor then says in the target language, "Stand," and stands up motioning for the students sitting on either side to rise.

Then, "Sit" and the instructor with the students sits down. Next, "Stand, Walk, Stop, Turn,..." etc. After hearing the commands several times and acting along with the students, the instructor sits down and invites individual students (including those observing in the audience) to perform alone in response to the commands. The intent is to demonstrate to each of the students that they have indeed internalized the strange utterances and understand them perfectly.

From the "big eight," unending combinations are possible to help students rapidly and gracefully internalize an intricate linguistic map of how the target language works. Examples of combinations that number in thousands of sentences starting with the "big eight" would be: "Stand, walk to the chalkboard and touch the eraser."

"Walk to the door, open it, and ask, "Who is there?"

"Run to the chalkboard, write your name, and under your name, write my name."

"If I walk to the table, and pick up a piece of paper, you run to the closet and get the broom."

Once understanding is achieved
and students begin to talk, then what?

Internalizing *understanding* of the phonology, morphology, and semantics of a target language is not a trivial achievement. It cannot be rushed. It will take time and patience. However, I can promise that if you use the language-body conversations of TPR, students will internalize the target language rapidly in huge chunks rather than word-by-word. The success of this procedure is a heady experience for both the instructor and the students. The instructor will feel enormous power and the students will feel that something magical is happening to them.

I can also promise that as the process of understanding through the body continues, at some point, each student will be *ready to talk*. This readiness to talk varies from student to student. A few will be ready almost immediately, others will not be ready for many weeks, but most seem to be eager to talk after 10 to 20 hours of TPR instruction. It is important to respect each student's decision as to when that person is ready to talk.

Again, this readiness cannot be forced by the instructor; it will appear spontaneously and when students begin to talk, it will not be perfect. There will be many distortions, but gradually, production will shape itself in the direction of the native speaker. Whether production will be accent-free is a function of age. Before puberty, the probability is extremely high that the student will be accent-free, but after puberty, the probability is almost certain that the individual will have some accent no matter how many years the person lives in the foreign country. (For more on this important issue, see Asher, 2000, and Garcia, 2001).

What can be done to accelerate the development of production

As language-body conversations continue, the student internalizes more and more details about the phonology, morphology and semantic structure of the target language. This internalization process proceeds in a kind of linguistic zero-gravity because the student seems to float in a weightlessness state. Each move seems effortless. The language code imprints at a rapid rate with an ease that gives the illusion that nothing has happened. When the internal linguistic map is imprinted with enough detail, talk is released analogous to the spontaneous appearance of speech in infants. As with the infant, speech is distorted, fragmented, and develops in slow-motion compared with the flashing speed the student has been internalizing comprehension.

Speech appears in "role reversal" after about 10 to 20 hours of TPR instruction. At this point, the instructor invites students who are ready, to assume the role of the instructor and utter commands to direct the behavior of fellow students and the instructor. In a search to accelerate the develop of production— that is, talking, reading, and writing, an experienced TPR instructor of Spanish, Blaine Ray, has successfully tested with his level 1 high school and college students a storytelling technique which he calls, *Look, I Can Talk*. This is a student textbook, now available in English, Spanish, French, and German, in which students listen and watch as the instructor tells an illustrated story in the target language using familiar vocabulary. Gestures are used to cue different words in the story such as a whistle and a slap on the thigh for dog and rubbing of the thumb and forefinger to represent money. Then, using gestures, each student is invited to retell the story in their own words to another student.

After that, each student writes the story using their own words. Rapidly, story by story, students are amazed to discover that they can express themselves in speech, reading and writing. You can order for your level 2 students, *Look, I Can Talk More!* in English, Spanish, French, and German and for level 3 students, *Look, I'm Still Talking*. Todd McKay has written and pretested for eight years a series of student books entitled, *TPR Storytelling: especially for students in elementary and middle school. (For more details on these books, see the pages in the back of this book.)*

Why most students experience success with TPR

As a hypothesis, it may be that most students are more right-brained in processing information. If so, then "school" as it is usually conducted, would not foster successful learning experiences. Hence, any instructional strategy that has built-in brainswitching should be successful with most students for first trial learning, long-term retention, and zero stress. Of course, that is exactly what TPR offers.

We have observed in the typical school population that students with a painful history of difficulties coping with academic content presented through the left brain, excel in language classes that apply TPR. For the first time in their school experience, these students achieve at the same level as the "A" students—the "smart kids." Ironically, these students who have "difficulty" learning are often "written off" by school administrators as "unteachable with low academic aptitude," and hence unprepared for the demands of foreign language classes. After all, they can't cope with classes in their native language, so how can we expect them to manage classes in a foreign language?

There is another powerful advantage to brainswitching instructional strategies especially in school where confinement restricts movement both physically and psychologically. Space is diminished to the territory around one's desk and left brain instruction draws the circle of space even tighter around the individual with the constraint of sitting in a chair, focusing attention and minimal body motion.

With TPR, space expands rather than contracts. Students are in motion using their bodies to respond to directions in the target language. There is instant success followed by nonstop assimilation of the target language. The interaction among students can continue for hours after the TPR class is over. Students can play with the target language using utterances to direct each other:

"Pass the ball to me."

"Come here!"

"Throw the ball to her!"

Stand over here!"

Walk forward three steps!"

Another exciting application of TPR is using the target language in coaching sport's activities. For example, all coaching for soccer could be in Arabic, Chinese, Spanish, or any other target language—because there is instant understanding with directions such as, "Pass the ball to Luke." "Stretch your arms like this to block the pass." "Jump higher!" Students not only improve their skill in a sport but as an additional bonus, acquire another language in the process.

Of course, this strategy of coaching in another language applies to instruction in any vocational skill. A cooking class, for instance, can be done in French as easily as English or Japanese, because directions are transparent to the trainees.

Application to teaching
mathematics and science

Skillful brainswitching from left to right and right to left is brain compatible instruction that reaches most students. For example, it is not enough to tell students (which is left brain input). *Telling* is the favorite mode of input from instructors. Code words for *telling* include "cover the chapter," or "explain" the concepts.

For example, ask a few people to give you the first thoughts that come into their minds when you say, "algebra." Typical responses are: pain, confusion, equations, unknowns, headache, tension, Xs and Ys. It is apparent from national test scores that "requiring" a course in algebra is not the equivalent of "acquiring" skill in algebra. *Requiring* is not the same as *acquiring*.

Algebra is a fundamental skill one needs to operate in higher mathematics, yet few high school graduates feel comfortable or proficient in using this powerful language. Not only do most graduates have zero competency, but they can see no value in this activity. It is perceived as an academic obstacle one must somehow hurdle to graduate. It is beyond the scope of this paper to explore the value of algebra except to hint that algebra is closer to theology than to engineering, an insight known for hundreds of years by spiritual teachers and the great philosophers. The reason, of course, is that the exquisite patterning of mathematics contradicts the randomness hypothesis of human existence. For example, the concept of evolution cannot explain the patterns within mathematics that fit together with a perfection that defies all "laws" of probability.

Consider this simple metaphor suggested by the prolific science writer, Isaac Asimov: If you shuffle a new deck of cards only once, how many times must you shuffle to return the cards to their original arrangement? The answer is that it will require billions of shuffles to get the cards back into the original sequence. If you disturb the arrangement of 52 items, it takes billions of trials to retrieve the initial pattern. In algebra, there are hundreds of items which fit together with astonishing perfection; hence to achieve that fit by randomness would require not billions of shuffles, not trillions of shuffles, but so *many* shuffles that we do not have an appropriate word in any language.

We attempt to explain the intricate biological patterns of humans, animals, plants, and even galaxies as the end-product of billions of years of imperceptible changes. But what about mathematics? There was no evolution. The labyrinth of patterns was discovered rather than invented. The patterns are there without an explanation of how they came to be.

But, let's return to the task of "learning" algebra. I can share a brainswitching strategy that helps all students internalize a simple model of algebra that is rich in meaning and enables them to perform successfully. It involves asking the students to stand up. I ask them to relax, move so that they have room between themselves and the person on either side. Then, I tell them that I know the picture they have as to what algebra is (because they just told me). "Now, let's compare that picture with the picture in my head. Algebra to me is *like flying an airplane*. Everybody extend your arms out from your body like this" and I demon-strate. "Notice that the plane is flying level. The object of algebra is to fly the plane level. You will know that the plane is level because the equal sign will light up on display panel in the cockpit."

"Now notice how your airplane maneuvers when I turn the wheel like this" (and I turn the imaginary wheel to one direc-tion). As I turn the wheel, students will automatically lower one arm and raise the other to represent that their planes are making a turn. Next, I say, "What will happen if the plane continues in this direction?"

A student will volunteer, "We will crash and burn!"

"That's right!" I respond. "Quickly, tell me what to do."

Another student will exclaim, "Turn the wheel in the oppo-site direction."

I do so, and the "wings" of the planes in the room move to a level position. "Ah, now we are safe again. The plane is flying level. You can put it on automatic pilot, take out your lunch, and relax."

"Let's make another turn," and we go through the maneuver in the opposite direction. "Notice that anytime you make a turn, the plane is in danger until you turn the wheel back to level the wings. *The object in algebra is always to fly the plane level.*"

Now the students have internalized a model in motion that I can refer to in any algebraic maneuver. For example, in $y - \hat{y} = x$, I will comment that the plane is flying level because the equal sign lit up on the display panel of the cockpit. But I want to turn the wheel by eliminating a minus $\hat{y}$. "Tell me how to do this."

Someone will advise me to, "Add $\hat{y}$ to the left side."

"Fine," I respond, "but show me with your body how the plane is flying" and the student will move one arm straight up in the air and the other sloping down. "Are we in danger of crash-ing?" I ask.

"Yes," a student responds.

"Quickly," I urge, "turn the wheel the other way to level the wings. What must I do?"

A student will help me with, "Add $\hat{y}$ to the right side."

The cockpit display now reads: $y = x + \hat{y}$. The plane is flying level. We are safe until we make another algebraic maneuver.

The Future of TPR

The most exciting application of TPR may be in Europe rather than America. The concept of a "United States of Europe" suggests that it may not be necessary for people in different European countries to "speak each other's language." It may be more realistic for each person trained with TPR instruction to only understand six or more other languages. Speaking those other languages is not necessary because, for instance, a person from England speaks English to someone from Italy and that individual responds in Italian. Everyone speaks in their native language which is most comfortable.

REFERENCES

Asher, James J. **Learning Another Language Through Actions,** Triple-Expanded Sixth Edition, Year 2000.
Sky Oaks Productions, Inc., P.O. Box 1102, Los Gatos, California, 95031.

Asher, James J. **The Super School of the 21st Century**.
Demonstrates how students of all ages enjoy fast, stress-free learning on the right side of the brain for *any subject* or *skill*.
Sky Oaks Productions, Inc., P.O. Box 1102, Los Gatos, California, 95031.

Asher, James J. "Year 2000 Update for the Total Physical Response, known worldwide as TPR." You can read this article on the web at: **www.tpr-world.com**

Asher, James J. "Year 2001 Update for the Total Physical Response, known worldwide as TPR." You can read this article on the web at: **www.tpr-world.com**

Cabello, Francisco. **Total Physical Response in the First Year.** (Can be ordered in English, Spanish, or French.) 2001, Sky Oaks Productions, Inc., P.O. Box 1102, Los Gatos, California, 95031.

Garcia, Ramiro. **Instructor's Notebook: How to Apply TPR for Best Results.** Fifth Edition, 2001, Sky Oaks Productions, Inc., P.O. Box 1102, Los Gatos, California 95031.

Krashen, Stephen D. "TPR: Still a Very Good Idea." Novelty, Volume 5, Number 4. December 1998. You can also read this article on the web at: http://ipisun.jpte.hu/~joe/novelty/krashen_98_december.html

Márquez, Nancy. **Learning with Movements: Total Physical Response English for Children,** 1999. Sky Oaks Productions, Inc., P.O. Box 1102, Los Gatos, California, 95031.

Márquez, Nancy. **Apprendiendo con Movimientos: Método TPR Español,** 1999. Sky Oaks Productions, Inc., P.O. Box 1102, Los Gatos, California, 95031.

Márquez, Nancy. **L'Enseignement Par Le Mouvement,** 1999. Sky Oaks Productions, Inc., P.O. Box 1102, Los Gatos, California, 95031.

McKay, Todd. **TPR Storytelling Especially for Students in Elementary and Middle School,** 2001. *Available in English, Spanish, or French.* Sky Oaks Productions, Inc., P.O. Box 1102, Los Gatos, California, 95031.

Ray, Blaine and Contee Seely. **Fluency Through TPR Storytelling.** Sky Oaks Productions, Inc., P.O. Box 1102, Los Gatos, California, 95031.)

Ray, Blaine. **Look, I Can Talk!** (level 1). **Look, I Can Talk More!** (level 2). **Look, I'm Still Talking!** (level 3). *Available in English, Spanish, French, or German.* Sky Oaks Productions, Inc., P.O. Box 1102, Los Gatos, California, 95031)

Schessler, Eric J. **English Grammar Through Actions**. How to TPR 50 grammatical features in English. Sky Oaks Productions, Inc., P.O. Box 1102, Los Gatos, California, 95031.

Schessler, Eric J. **Spanish Grammar Through Actions**. How to TPR 50 grammatical features in Spanish. Sky Oaks Productions, Inc., P.O. Box 1102, Los Gatos, California, 95031.

Schessler, Eric J. **French Grammar Through Actions**. How to TPR 50 grammatical features in French. Sky Oaks Productions, Inc., P.O. Box 1102, Los Gatos, California, 95031.

Seely, Contee **TPR Is More Than Commands At All Levels.** Sky Oaks Productions, Inc., P.O. Box 1102, Los Gatos, California, 95031.

Silvers, Stephen M. **Listen and Perform: TPR for Elementary and Middle School Children**. (You can order this book in English, Spanish or French.) Sky Oaks Productions, Inc., P.O. Box 1102, Los Gatos, California, 95031.

Silvers, Stephen M. **Listen and Perform: Teacher's Guidebook**. Sky Oaks Productions, Inc., P.O. Box 1102, Los Gatos, California, 95031.

Silvers, Stephen M. **The Command Book: How to TPR 2,000 Vocabulary Items in Any Language**. Sky Oaks Productions, Inc., P.O. Box 1102, Los Gatos, California, 95031.

Wolfe, David and G. Jones. 1982. "Integrating Total Physical Response strategy in a level 1 Spanish class." *Foreign Language Annals* 14:273-80.

Woodruff-Wieding, Margaret S. and Laura J. Ayala. **Favorite Games for FL-ESL Classes**. Sky Oaks Productions, Inc., P.O. Box 1102, Los Gatos, California, 95031.

Expanded 6th Edition!
Our Best Seller !!

✓ **Demonstrates** step-by-step **how to apply TPR** to help children and adults acquire another language **without stress.**

✓ More than **150 hours** of **classroom-tested TPR lessons** that **can be adapted to teaching any language** including Arabic, Chinese, English, French, German, Hebrew, Japanese, Russian, and Spanish.

Learning Another Language
Through Actions

by
James J. Asher
Originator of the

World Famous

Total Physical Response

Year 2000 ❖ 6th Edition
Over 50,000 Copies in Print!

✓ A behind-the-scenes look at how **TPR** was developed.

✓ **Answers more than 100 frequently asked questions** about **TPR.**

✓ **Easy to understand** summary of 25 years of research with Dr. Asher's world famous **Total Physical Response**.

NEW FEATURES IN THE YEAR 2000 6TH EDITION
- Frequently Asked Questions - Newly Expanded!
- Letters from my mailbag
- e-mail addresses for TPR instructors around the world

Triple Expanded 4th Edition!
—Best Seller—

The Graphics Book©

For Students of All Ages acquiring
English, Spanish, French, or German

by RAMIRO GARCIA

Dear Colleague;

You recall that I introduced graphics in the **Instructor's Notebook.** Hundreds of teachers discovered that **students of all ages** thoroughly enjoyed working with the material.

Your students understand a huge chunk of the target language because you used TPR. Now, with my new *graphics* book, you can follow up with ***300 drawings*** on tear-out strips that help your students *zoom ahead* with **more vocabulary, grammar, talking, reading** and **writing** in the target language.

In this book, you will receive **step-by-step guidance** in how to apply the *graphics* effectively with **children and adults** acquiring <u>**any**</u> **language** including **ESL.**

As an **extra bonus**, I provide you with **60 multiple-choice graphic tests for beginning and intermediate students.** Order **The Graphics Book** directly from the publisher, Sky Oaks Productions in your choice of English, Spanish, French or German.

Order from anywhere in the world with your Visa/Mastercard, check, money order, or official school purchase order.
Sky Oaks Productions, Inc. P.O. Box 1102, Los Gatos, CA 95031 USA • Phone: (408) 395-7600 • Fax: (408) 395-8440

TPR BINGO©
by RAMIRO GARCIA

In 25 years of applying the **Total Physical Response** in my high school and adult Spanish classes, **TPR Bingo** is the one game that students ask to play over and over!

When playing the game, students hear the instructor utter directions in the target language. As they advance in

Use your Visa or Mastercard to order from anywhere in the world • We ship ASAP!

understanding, individual students ask to play the role of caller, which gives them valuable practice in **reading and speaking.** For an extra bonus, students **internalize numbers** in the target language from 1 through 100.

TPR Bingo comes with complete step-by-step directions for playing the game and rules for winning. There are 40 play-boards (one side for beginners and the reverse side for advanced students). A master caller's board is included, with 100 pictures, chips, and caller-cards in your choice of English, Spanish, French or German. As I tell my colleagues, "Try this game with your students. You will love it—they will love it!"

Brand-new feature!
Now included in every order of TPR Bingo...
Play TPR Bingo with your students to move them from the imperative to the declarative (and interrogative). It's easy, it's fun, and you will love it!

How to TPR Vocabulary!

NEWS FLASH!

The popular TPR book, **Learning With Movements** by Nancy Márquez is available in **English, Spanish,** and now **French.**

The unique features are:

- A marvelously **simple format** which allows you to glance at a page and instantly generate one direction after another to move your students rapidly in a logical series of actions.
- An **initial screening test** will give you a realistic concept of each student's skill.
- After each lesson, there is a **competency test** for individual students.
- Recommended for preschool and elementary students in **any language**, including the sign language of the deaf.

Hot off the press in your choice of *English, Spanish,* or *French!*

Dear Colleague:

I want to share with you the **TPR Lessons** that my high school and college students **thoroughly enjoy** and **retain** for weeks—even months later. My book has...

- A script you may follow step-by-step including a list of props needed to conduct each class.
- A command format that gives students **instant success.** (Students show their understanding of the target language by responding to directions uttered by the instructor. **Production** is delayed until students are ready and feel comfortable.)
- Grammar taught implicitly through the imperative.
- Tests for an evaluation of student achievement.

TOTAL PHYSICAL RESPONSE IN THE FIRST YEAR

By
FRANCISCO L. CABELLO
with William Denevan

Sincerely,

Francisco Cabello

FAVORITE GAMES
FOR
FL - ESL CLASSES

(For All Levels and All Languages)
by Laura Ayala & Dr. Margaret Woodruff-Wieding

Chapter 1: Introduction

Chapter 2: Getting Started with Games
- How to get students involved
- How the games were selected or invented.

Chapter 3: Game Learning Categories
- Alphabet and Spelling
- Changing Case
- Changing Voice
- Describing Objects
- Getting Acquainted
- Giving Commands
- Hearing and Pronouncing
- Statements & Questions
- Negating Sentences
- Numbers and Counting
- Parts of the Body and Grooming
- Plurals and Telling How Many
- Changing Tense
- Describing Actions

- Possessive Adjectives & Belonging
- Recognizing Related Words
- Telling Time
- Using Correct Word Order.

Chapter 4: Games by Technique
- Responding to Commands
- Guessing
- Simulating
- Listing
- Categorizing
- Associating
- Sequencing
- Matching

Chapter 5: Special Materials For Games
- Objects
- Authentic Props
- Pictures
- Cards
- Stories

Chapter 6: Bibliography

Winner of the Paul Pimsleur Award!

Here are **detailed lesson plans** for **60 hours** of **TPR Instruction** that make it **easy** for novice instructors to apply the **total physical response** approach **at any level**. The **TPR lessons** include

- **Step-by-step directions** so that instructors **in any language** (including ESL) can apply comprehension training successfully.

- **Competency tests** to be given after the 10th and 30th lessons.

- **Pre-tested short exercises:** dozens to capture student interest.

- **Many photographs**

COMPREHENSION BASED LANGUAGE LESSONS
LEVEL 1
By
Margaret S. Woodruff, Ph.D.
Winner of the Paul Pimsleur Award
(With Dr. Janet King Swaffar)

NOTE! We have printed the lessons in two languages: **English** and **German**, but we have charged you only the cost of printing a single language.

TPR Storytelling

by Todd McKay

✔ Pre-tested in the classroom for 8 years to guarantee success for your students.

✔ Easy to follow, step-by-step guidance each day for three school years - one year at a time.

✔ Todd shows you how to switch from activity to activity to keep the novelty alive for your students day after day.

✔ Evidence shows the approach works: Kids in storytelling class outperformed kids in the traditional ALM class.

✔ Each story comes illustrated with snazzy cartoons that appeal to children.

✔ There is continuity to the story line because the stories revolve around one family.

✔ Complete with tests to assess comprehension, speaking, reading and writing.

✔ Yes, cultural topics are included.

✔ Yes, stories include most of the content you will find in traditional textbooks, including vocabulary and grammar.

✔ Yes, included is a brief refresher of classic TPR, by the originator-Dr. James J. Asher.

✔ Yes, games are included.

✔ Yes, your students will have the long-term retention you expect from TPR instructions.

✔ Todd includes his e-mail address to answer your questions if you get stuck along the way.

New TPR Products by Todd McKay:

• Illustrated student booklet for Year One, Year Two, or Year Three. (All three booklets available in **English**, **Spanish**, or **French**.)

• Teacher's Guidebook

• Complete Testing Packet for listening comprehension, speaking, reading, and writing.

• Transparencies

• Video Demonstration to show you how to perform successfully every step in the Teacher's Guidebook.

Best Demonstrations of Classic TPR Anywhere in the World!

James J. Asher's Classic Videos demonstrate the original research...

Historic videos show the original TPR research by Dr. James J. Asher with children and adults learning Japanese, Spanish, French and German. We include with every video cassette a copy of the scientific publications documenting the amazing results you will see. A must for anyone teaching TPR. Each video cassette is unique, and shows different stress-free features of TPR instruction — *no matter what language you are teaching,* including English as a Second Language. *(Each video is narrated in English.)*

Children Learning Another Language: An Innovative Approach©

VHS, Color, 26 minutes, shows the excitement of children from K through 6th grades as they acquire **Spanish** and **French** with **TPR**. (ESL students will enjoy this too!)

If you are searching for ways that motivate children to learn another language, don't miss this classic video demonstration. The ideas you will see can be applied in your classroom for any grade level and for any language, including English as a second language.

A Motivational Strategy for Language Learning©

VHS, Color, 25 minutes, demonstrates step-by-step how to apply **TPR** for best results with students between the ages of 17 and 60 acquiring **Spanish**. Easy to see how **TPR** can be used to teach any target language.

See the excitement on the faces of students as they understand everything the instructor is saying in Spanish. After several weeks in which the students are silent, but responding rapidly to commands in Spanish, students spontaneously begin to talk. You will see the amazing transition from understanding to speaking, reading, and writing!

Strategy for Second Language Learning©

VHS, Color, 19 minutes, shows students from 17 to 60 acquiring **German** with **TPR**. Applies to *any* language!

Even when the class meets only two nights a week and no homework is required, the retention of spoken German is remarkable. You will be impressed by the graceful transition from understanding to speaking, reading, and writing!

Demonstration of a New Strategy in Language Learning©

VHS, B&W, 15 minutes, shows American children acquiring **Japanese** with **TPR**. Applies to *any* language! You will see the first demonstration of the **Total Physical Response** ever recorded on film when American children rapidly internalize a complex sample of Japanese. You will also see the astonishing retention one year later! Narrated by the Originator of TPR, James J. Asher.

NOTES:

NOTES:

NOTES: